PREVIOUSLY IN *THE SECRET OF THE SWORDFISH:*

FOLLOWING THE SURPRISE ATTACK BY THE FORCES OF USURPER BASAM DAMDU, CAPTAIN BLAKE OF THE BRITISH INTELLIGENCE SERVICE AND PROFESSOR MORTIMER WERE FORCED TO HURRIEDLY ESCAPE THE SCAFELL FACTORY ABOARD THE GOLDEN ROCKET IN ORDER TO MAKE THEIR WAY TO A SECRET BASE AND ALLOW MORTIMER TO FINISH HIS WORK ON A NEW 'ULTIMATE WEAPON': THE SWORDFISH...

...AS THE ARMOURED CAR SHELLS BLAKE AND MORTIMER'S REFUGE, THE CANYON IS SUDDENLY FILLED WITH THE SOUND OF HEAVY GUNFIRE...

THE BEZENDJAS HASN'T RELAXED HIS SURVEILLANCE AND...

E. P. JACOBS

THE SECRET OF THE SWORDFISH

PART 3
SX1 STRIKES BACK

Colour work: Philippe Biermé, Luce Daniels

467 503 86 6

Original title: Le secret de l'espadon V3

Original edition: © Editions Blake & Mortimer / Studio Jacobs (Dargaud – Lombard s.a.) 1986
by E.P. Jacobs
www.dargaud.com
All rights reserved

English translation: © 2013 Cinebook Ltd

Translator: Jerome Saincantin
Lettering and text layout: Design Amorandi
Printed in Spain by Just Colour Graphic

This edition first published in Great Britain in 2013 by
Cinebook Ltd
56 Beech Avenue
Canterbury, Kent
CT4 7TA
www.cinebook.com

A CIP catalogue record for this book
is available from the British Library

ISBN 978-1-84918-174-7

9th CINEBOOK
The 9th Art Publisher

ALL AT ONCE A PIECE OF ROCK BREAKS OFF AND BLAKE IS THROWN OFF THE LEDGE!...

RAISING HIS PISTOLS, MORTIMER EMPTIES BOTH MAGAZINES TOWARDS THE PROJECTOR.

A CODED MESSAGE SENT BY MORTIMER WHILE IN CAPTIVITY ALLOWED BLAKE AND NASIR
TO LOCATE AND RECOVER THE PLANS...

IN THE SKIES OVER LHASA, NEW CAPITAL OF THE GREAT WORLD EMPIRE, THE RED WING II, COLONEL OLRIK'S PERSONAL PLANE, HAS JUST APPEARED...

'WELL, WELL, AREN'T YOU THE ONE WHO WAS WORKING ON THE FENCE THE OTHER DAY?...' SAID OLRIK SUDDENLY, STARING INQUISITIVELY AT NASIR.

A MONTH AFTER THESE DRAMATIC EVENTS, A TRAIN IS IDLING AT KARACHI STATION. IT'S A CONVOY OF INTELLECTUALS AND TECHNICIANS BOUND FOR ONE OF THE SINISTER CONCENTRATION CAMPS OF THE HIMALAYAS.

Ah! Finally, we're about done!

By the way, I saw Li this morning. He seemed quite depressed by this endless inquiry into Mortimer's escape...

A bad deal for Olrik, that business.

Yes... And just between ourselves, I heard that Dr Fo accused Olrik — before the Great Council — of double dealings and of trying to obtain the plans of the Swordfish for himself. The colonel protested, of course. However, he hasn't left his residence since he came back from Lhasa, and the guard around it has been increased... By order of the Emperor, apparently...

House arrest, eh?

MEANWHILE, INSIDE ONE OF THE WAGONS, A GROUP OF PRISONERS IS DISCUSSING THE EVENTS...

... It's like I tell you, mates: a real adventure novel! Lifted first by a helicopter, then by a submarine! In Karachi! Under Olrik's nose! The Imperials spared no expense: destroyers, planes, radars, the lot — and yet, despite all that, pfwt! Gone! Vanished!

So, do you think the submarine managed to escape out to sea and...

AT THAT MOMENT, THE DOOR SLAMS OPEN AND THE GUARDS USE THEIR RIFLE BUTTS TO PUSH A MAN IN RATHER POOR SHAPE INTO THE WAGON.

Have a nice trip!

Where do you come from, friend?

My name's Bell, Donald Bell. I was in Karachi for business. I'd managed to hide until now, but...

Donald Bell?... Are you Bell the engineer from the Atomic Energy Commission, by any chance?

What? You know me?

No, but I know your brother very well, Lieutenant Archie Bell. He often spoke about you! Nice to meet you, Bell!... Oh, but I forgot... Jack Harper, former district chief in the north...

Well, I'll be!... What a surprise!

Hey, Harper, take a look at what I just found under the straw...

Ah, an iron lever! That may well come in handy...

BUT THE BLOW OF A WHISTLE SIGNALS THE DEPARTURE OF THE CONVOY. THE LOCOMOTIVE IS PRECEDED BY A SAND-FILLED WAGON DESTINED TO BEAR THE BRUNT OF ANY MINE EXPLOSION...

TOOOT

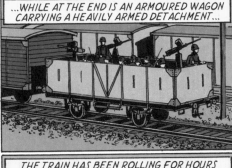

...WHILE AT THE END IS AN ARMOURED WAGON CARRYING A HEAVILY ARMED DETACHMENT...

THE TRAIN HAS BEEN ROLLING FOR HOURS UNDER A SCORCHING SUN...

...WHEN TOWARDS THE END OF THE DAY, JUST AS IT'S ENTERING A NARROW PASS, A POWERFUL EXPLOSION BLOWS THE FRONT WAGON TO SMITHEREENS.

BANG

THE TRAIN COMES TO A SUDDEN HALT AND THE SHOOTING BEGINS. THE DRIVER ATTEMPTS TO REVERSE THE ENGINE BUT HIS EFFORTS ARE FOILED, AS ONE OF THE CONNECTING RODS HAS BEEN FOULED BY DEBRIS FROM THE EXPLOSION. THE CONVOY IS PARALYSED.

LOCKED INSIDE THE WAGONS, THE PRISONERS DO THEIR BEST TO FOLLOW THE STAGES OF THE SKIRMISH.

An attack by partisans, no doubt!

...Sounds heated!...

Hmm! This won't be easy, Sergeant...

No, sir, it won't... It's that blooming wagon that enables them to hold!

DESPITE ULTIMATELY FAILING, THE ATTEMPT TO RETREAT HAS INDEED MANAGED TO BRING THE ARMOURED WAGON OUT OF THE NARROW DEFILE IT HAD ENTERED, ALLOWING IT TO SWEEP THE SURROUNDINGS WITH WITHERING FIRE.

Hey, Harper, isn't this a good time to use our lever? We should be able to lift the floorboards with it!

Ah! Now there's a fine idea, Bell!

SOON, THANKS TO HARPER'S VIGOROUS EFFORTS, THE FLOOR BEGINS TO GIVE WAY...

Hold it tight!

Go ahead, Jack! It's moving!...

Blast it! We can't afford to wait around. Their air force could fall on us at any moment!

Sir, with your permission, I'm going to end this... A lone man has a better chance of getting to grenade range.

All right, Mac, but watch yourself...

MEANWHILE, HARPER AND HIS COMPANIONS, HAVING TORN A HOLE THROUGH THE FLOOR, LOWER THEMSELVES TO THE RAILS.

Careful! The armoured wagon is just behind ours!

MAC, WHO'S CRAWLED TO THE FOOT OF THE EMBANKMENT, GRABS A GRENADE AND PULLS OUT THE PIN.

UNFORTUNATELY, FROM THEIR HIGH VANTAGE POINT, THE IMPERIALS HAVE SEEN THE SERGEANT AND UNDERSTOOD HIS INTENTIONS...

Look out! He's stopped... Don't miss him!... Quick!...

Don't worry, Lieutenant...

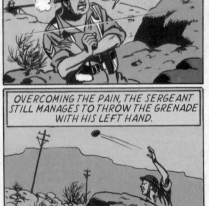

A HAIL OF BULLETS SWIFTLY HAMMERS THE ROCK BEHIND WHICH MAC IS SHELTERING. ONE OF THEM HITS HIM IN THE ARM...

OW!

OVERCOMING THE PAIN, THE SERGEANT STILL MANAGES TO THROW THE GRENADE WITH HIS LEFT HAND.

UNFORTUNATELY, THROWN WITH LESS STRENGTH, THE WEAPON LANDS ON THE BALLAST LESS THAN TWO FEET AWAY FROM THE TERRIFIED FUGITIVES...

BUT BELL, WITH LIGHTNING-FAST REFLEXES, GRABS THE GRENADE...

...AND, JUMPING TO HIS FEET, THROWS IT OVER THE WAGON'S ARMOURED SIDE!

THE DEVASTATING EXPLOSION ELIMINATES THE ENTIRE DEFENSIVE FORCE INSTANTLY...

Forward!

AND THE COMMANDOES CHARGE...

Hurrah!

Good work, gentlemen!

Lieutenant, this is Donald Bell, the man of the hour!

My congratulations, sir! We really are in your debt. If you hadn't kept your cool, I'm afraid we might have had to fall back!

Bah! I didn't have much choice, Lieutenant.

MEANWHILE, THE COMMANDOES HAVE QUICKLY FREED THE PRISONERS FROM THE OTHER WAGONS.

Well, Mac? The arm?

Nothing serious, sir! A mere scratch!

A SHORT WHILE LATER, PRISONERS AND COMMANDOES LEAVE THE SINISTER TRAIN AND SCRAMBLE DOWN THE EMBANKMENT.

Come on! Hurry up!

AFTER A MILE AND A HALF OF HARD MARCHING, THE TROOP REACHES A STEEP-SIDED ROAD WHERE SEVERAL MILITARY TRUCKS ARE WAITING...

Remember your orders! Fifty yards between trucks. No lights, obviously, and as much speed as possible! We must reach point H before dawn. There we will refuel, rest and wait for the night before we go on. Keep your eyes peeled and be careful. We're in enemy territory; the slightest mechanical incident could prove fatal! Understood?

Understood, sir!

And now, Bell, on to freedom!

Heaven hears you, Jack!

WHILE THE SUN'S LAST RAYS FLARE BRIEFLY ON THE HORIZON, THE COLUMN DRIVES OFF IN A CLOUD OF DUST.

TWO DAYS LATER, AFTER A PERILOUS TREK, THE COMMANDO REACHES THE CLIFFS OF MAKRAN. THE TRUCKS ARE HIDDEN AND CAMOUFLAGED IN A SAFE SPOT THEN THE TROOP TRAVELS ON TOWARDS THE BASE, ON FOOT THIS TIME...

...BEFORE STOPPING AT NIGHTFALL AT THE SPOT WHERE BLAKE AND NASIR DISAPPEARED WHEN MORTIMER WAS CAPTURED.

Gentlemen, listen carefully to my instructions, as your lives depend on it!... We are going to cross to the entrance of our base, which on this side is only accessible at low tide. You are therefore going to follow in single file, and very precisely, the path I am going to take. My men will install themselves among you for added safety. Anyone who deviates from the trail will inevitably fall into the extremely dangerous quicksand that guard the area surrounding that rock you see over there.

AND SLOWLY, CAUTIOUSLY, THE MEN START WALKING.

HAVING SAFELY NAVIGATED THE TREACHEROUS AREA, THE LIEUTENANT STOPS BEFORE ONE OF THE MANY CRACKS THAT RUN THROUGH THE ROCK.

Is everyone here?

Yes, sir!

WALKING TO THE BACK OF THE CRACK, THE OFFICER HALTS BEFORE THE INVISIBLE BARRIER FORMED BY A CAESIUM-BASED ELECTRIC EYE AND BEGINS TRACING MYSTERIOUS SIGNS IN THE AIR.

BY INTERCEPTING THE INVISIBLE BEAMS AT A PREDETERMINED RHYTHM, HE FORMS THE COMMANDOS' IDENTIFICATION SIGNAL ON THE CONTROL PANEL OF THE GUARD STATION.

Hello! This is guard station — Makran sector. Commando at door one. Everything normal. Open and turn the lights on!

IMMEDIATELY, THERE IS A FAINT CLICK AND THE ROCK FACE THAT WAS PROTECTED BY THE INVISIBLE BEAMS RISES, UNCOVERING AN ILLUMINATED PASSAGE...

This way!

THE GROUP ENTER IT AND EMERGE INTO A HUGE CAVE, BRILLIANTLY LIT AND FILLED WITH THE MURMUR OF WATER...

By Jove, Bell! What a prodigious sight! Look over there!...

Yes, yes, but don't get too close!...

Hey! Be careful!... The ground is treacherous and...

AT THAT INSTANT, HARPER'S FOOT SLIPS ON THE SLIMY ROCK...

Jack!!!

BUT BELL, AT THE RISK OF BEING PULLED DOWN HIMSELF, MANAGES TO GRAB HOLD OF THE UNLUCKY ONE AT THE LAST SECOND...

Well, old boy! I'd have taken quite a dive if it weren't for you!

Bah! You'd have got off with no worse than a forced bath. Still...

A forced bath?... Well, I wouldn't encourage you to try one... Have a look...

HAVING PICKED UP A FRAGMENT OF ROCK, THE LIEUTENANT THROWS IT INTO THE STAGNANT WATER.

PLOOSH

A DANTEAN SIGHT SUDDENLY APPEARS BEFORE THEIR EYES...

Well, gentlemen? What do you think?

That's horrific!!!

Heavens!

THE ROCK LANDED IN THE MIDDLE OF A SQUIRMING MASS OF HIDEOUS SPIDER CRABS THAT WERE LYING IN AMBUSH IN THE MUDDY BOTTOM STRADDLED BY THE STONY ARCH. THE DREADFUL BEASTS SCATTER WITH SINISTER SCREECHING...

TRANSFIXED, THE MEN CANNOT TEAR THEMSELVES AWAY FROM THE INCREDIBLE VISION.

To fall into that...!!!

No point in letting your imagination run wild, it's not good for the nerves. Come on, let's not linger here any longer, it's too damp. Onwards!

AFTER THAT UNSETTLING INCIDENT, THE MEN QUICKLY PASS THE CRAB PIT AND FOLLOW THEIR GUIDES DOWN A MAZE OF FANTASTICALLY SHAPED GALLERIES AND ROOMS...

...WHILE ON HIS SCREEN THE SENTRY FOLLOWS THEIR PROGRESSION STEP BY STEP, THANKS TO THE BARRIERS OF INVISIBLE BEAMS SCATTERED ALONG THEIR PATH.

BRIDGE

GANG-WAY

RAILWAY

2ND MS. DOOR

AT LAST THE GROUP REACH A FLIGHT OF STEPS, BARRED A SHORT WAY UP BY A MASSIVE STEEL DOOR.

BUT, LIKE THE FIRST DOOR, THIS RISES AS THEY APPROACH. AN ELECTRIC TRAIN IS WAITING THERE FOR THEM...

Hello!

13

Nice to see you again, sir. We were starting to fear the worst back at base...

I imagine you were; but it was no walk in the park! The buggers are starting to get organised...

THE TRAIN GETS UNDERWAY...

Go on, Phil!

...AND SPEEDS OFF TOWARDS THE HEART OF THE SECRET BASE.

INSIDE THE CARRIAGES, THE MEN IMMEDIATELY ENGAGE IN CONVERSATION ...

I must say, Lieutenant, this is like a dream!

A hundred fathoms under the sea, gentlemen...

Where are we right now?

What?...

You mean....?

Exactly. At the moment we're travelling at 40 miles per hour underneath the Strait of Hormuz...

Incredible!... And where are we heading to?...

Simply towards Ras Musandam.

Fantastic!... And this tunnel was excavated?

Oh no! There was already a sort of gallery formed by God knows what kind of geological convulsion; but it had to be converted, drained, consolidated, or widened in some sections. It wasn't an easy job, believe you me!

...Yes, gentlemen!... From the cliffs of Makran to the rocks of the Arabian Peninsula: 38 miles below the sea!

Blimey!

Tell me, it's sturdy and safe, right? 'Cause I can't swim!

...WHERE THE ENORMOUS STEEL GATE LIFTS UP TO ALLOW IT PASSAGE. SLOWING DOWN, THE TRAIN ENTERS THE SPACE...

...AND KEEPS GOING TOWARDS THE CENTRAL HALL. THE SENTRY, MEANWHILE, CONTACTS THE BASE'S COMMAND POST...

Hello! Hello! This is guard station – Makran sector...

...Lieutenant Brady's commando has just returned. Mission accomplished!... The men are being directed to the central hall...

14

SLOWING DOWN, THE TRAIN PASSES BENEATH THE MASSIVE STEEL GATE THAT HAS JUST RISEN TO ALLOW IT PASSAGE TOWARDS THE VERY HEART OF THE SECRET BASE!...

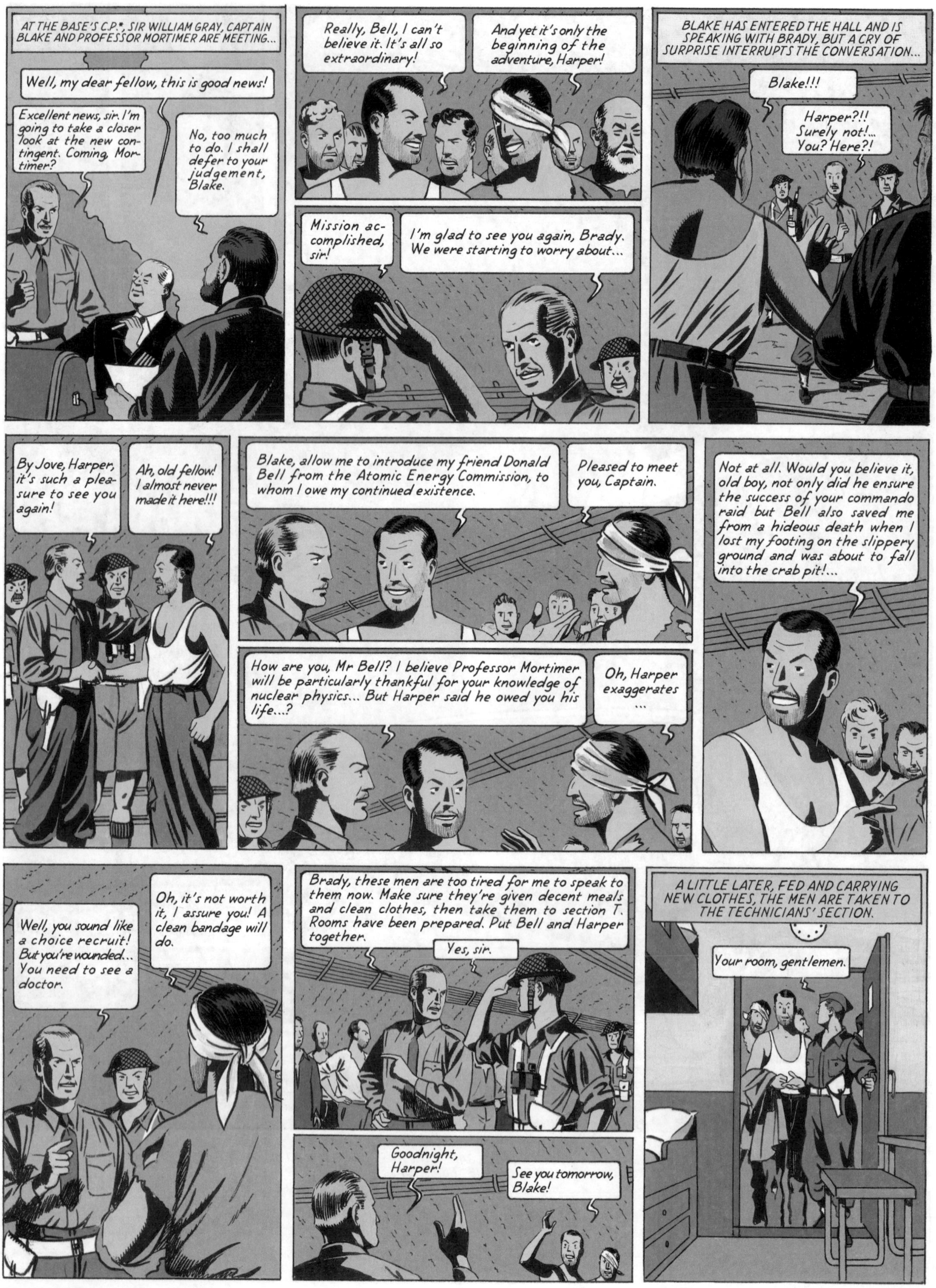

AT THE BASE'S C.P.*, SIR WILLIAM GRAY, CAPTAIN BLAKE AND PROFESSOR MORTIMER ARE MEETING...
Well, my dear fellow, this is good news!
Excellent news, sir. I'm going to take a closer look at the new contingent. Coming, Mortimer?
No, too much to do. I shall defer to your judgement, Blake.
Really, Bell, I can't believe it. It's all so extraordinary!
And yet it's only the beginning of the adventure, Harper!
Mission accomplished, sir!
I'm glad to see you again, Brady. We were starting to worry about...
BLAKE HAS ENTERED THE HALL AND IS SPEAKING WITH BRADY, BUT A CRY OF SURPRISE INTERRUPTS THE CONVERSATION...
Blake!!!
Harper?!! Surely not!... You? Here?!
By Jove, Harper, it's such a pleasure to see you again!
Ah, old fellow! I almost never made it here!!!
Blake, allow me to introduce my friend Donald Bell from the Atomic Energy Commission, to whom I owe my continued existence.
Pleased to meet you, Captain.
How are you, Mr Bell? I believe Professor Mortimer will be particularly thankful for your knowledge of nuclear physics... But Harper said he owed you his life...?
Oh, Harper exaggerates ...
Not at all. Would you believe it, old boy, not only did he ensure the success of your commando raid but Bell also saved me from a hideous death when I lost my footing on the slippery ground and was about to fall into the crab pit!...
Well, you sound like a choice recruit! But you're wounded... You need to see a doctor.
Oh, it's not worth it, I assure you! A clean bandage will do.
Brady, these men are too tired for me to speak to them now. Make sure they're given decent meals and clean clothes, then take them to section T. Rooms have been prepared. Put Bell and Harper together.
Yes, sir.
Goodnight, Harper!
See you tomorrow, Blake!
A LITTLE LATER, FED AND CARRYING NEW CLOTHES, THE MEN ARE TAKEN TO THE TECHNICIANS' SECTION.
Your room, gentlemen.

*COMMAND POST

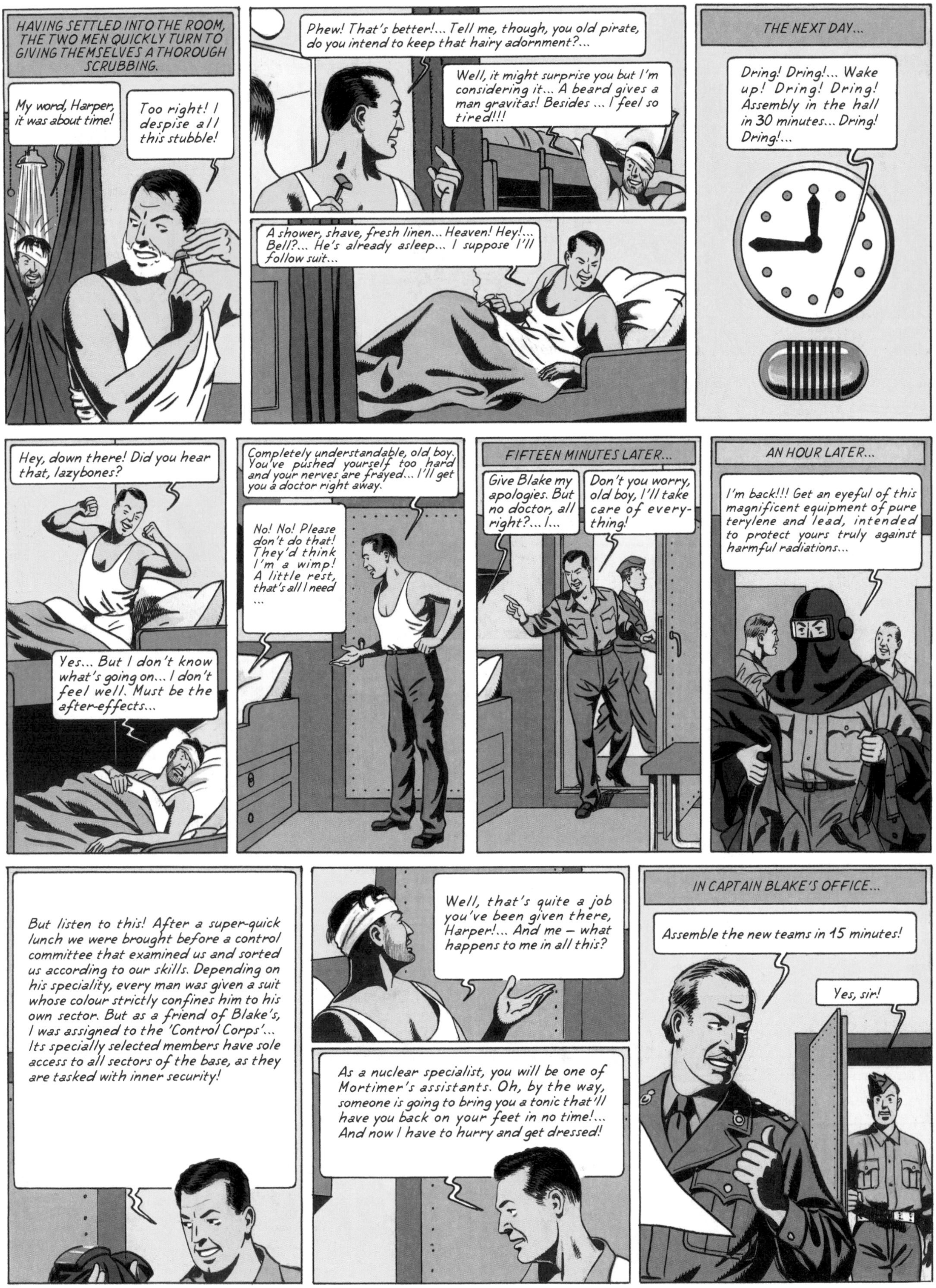
HAVING SETTLED INTO THE ROOM, THE TWO MEN QUICKLY TURN TO GIVING THEMSELVES A THOROUGH SCRUBBING.
My word, Harper, it was about time!
Too right! I despise all this stubble!
Phew! That's better!... Tell me, though, you old pirate, do you intend to keep that hairy adornment?...
Well, it might surprise you but I'm considering it... A beard gives a man gravitas! Besides ... I feel so tired!!!
A shower, shave, fresh linen... Heaven! Hey!... Bell?... He's already asleep... I suppose I'll follow suit...
THE NEXT DAY...
Dring! Dring!... Wake up! Dring! Dring! Assembly in the hall in 30 minutes... Dring! Dring!...
Hey, down there! Did you hear that, lazybones?
Yes... But I don't know what's going on... I don't feel well. Must be the after-effects...
Completely understandable, old boy. You've pushed yourself too hard and your nerves are frayed... I'll get you a doctor right away.
No! No! Please don't do that! They'd think I'm a wimp! A little rest, that's all I need ...
FIFTEEN MINUTES LATER...
Give Blake my apologies. But no doctor, all right?... I...
Don't you worry, old boy, I'll take care of everything!
AN HOUR LATER...
I'm back!!! Get an eyeful of this magnificent equipment of pure terylene and lead, intended to protect yours truly against harmful radiations...
But listen to this! After a super-quick lunch we were brought before a control committee that examined us and sorted us according to our skills. Depending on his speciality, every man was given a suit whose colour strictly confines him to his own sector. But as a friend of Blake's, I was assigned to the 'Control Corps'... Its specially selected members have sole access to all sectors of the base, as they are tasked with inner security!
Well, that's quite a job you've been given there, Harper!... And me – what happens to me in all this?
As a nuclear specialist, you will be one of Mortimer's assistants. Oh, by the way, someone is going to bring you a tonic that'll have you back on your feet in no time!... And now I have to hurry and get dressed!
IN CAPTAIN BLAKE'S OFFICE...
Assemble the new teams in 15 minutes!
Yes, sir!

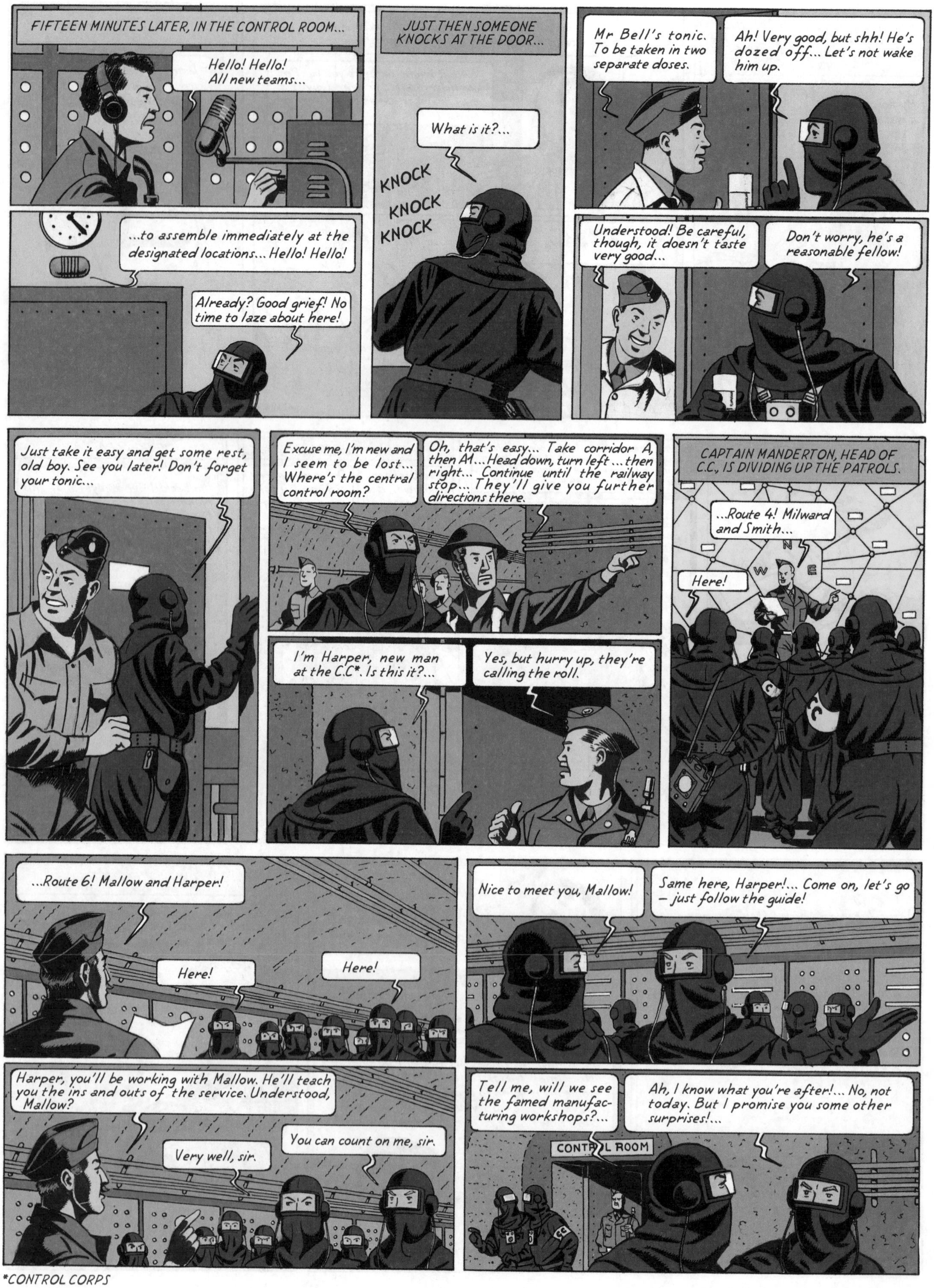
FIFTEEN MINUTES LATER, IN THE CONTROL ROOM...
Hello! Hello! All new teams...
...to assemble immediately at the designated locations... Hello! Hello!
Already? Good grief! No time to laze about here!
JUST THEN SOMEONE KNOCKS AT THE DOOR...
What is it?...
KNOCK
KNOCK
KNOCK
Mr Bell's tonic. To be taken in two separate doses.
Ah! Very good, but shh! He's dozed off... Let's not wake him up.
Understood! Be careful, though, it doesn't taste very good...
Don't worry, he's a reasonable fellow!
Just take it easy and get some rest, old boy. See you later! Don't forget your tonic...
Excuse me, I'm new and I seem to be lost... Where's the central control room?
Oh, that's easy... Take corridor A, then A1... Head down, turn left ... then right... Continue until the railway stop... They'll give you further directions there.
I'm Harper, new man at the C.C*. Is this it?...
Yes, but hurry up, they're calling the roll.
CAPTAIN MANDERTON, HEAD OF C.C., IS DIVIDING UP THE PATROLS.
...Route 4! Milward and Smith...
Here!
...Route 6! Mallow and Harper!
Here!
Here!
Nice to meet you, Mallow!
Same here, Harper!... Come on, let's go – just follow the guide!
Harper, you'll be working with Mallow. He'll teach you the ins and outs of the service. Understood, Mallow?
Very well, sir.
You can count on me, sir.
Tell me, will we see the famed manufacturing workshops?...
Ah, I know what you're after!... No, not today. But I promise you some other surprises!...
CONTROL ROOM

*CONTROL CORPS

QUICKLY CROSSING THE CENTRAL HALL, MALLOW AND HIS COMPANION HEAD TOWARDS THE LIFT THAT SERVES THEIR SECTOR.

What do we do?

Let me explain that...

There are infrared control points dotted along our route, and we have to tag them as we go. But apart from this security role, our main task is to detect any trace of suspicious radioactivity using this ultra-sensitive Geiger counter, and locate the source as rapidly as possible. We also stay in permanent contact with the control room...

...through our little low-frequency walkie-talkies. When we want to communicate with the C.P. or one of the other patrols, all we have to do is turn on the microphone and bring the device close to any metallic conductor that runs near the person you wish to reach. Moreover, an external microphone enables us to speak to people not equipped with walkie-talkies... But here we are.

MALLOW STEPS INTO THE DOORWAY AND WAVES A FEW SIGNS IN FRONT OF THE ELECTRIC EYE CONTROLLING THE DIVING SUITS CHAMBER.

Hello! This is Harper, our newest recruit...

Hello!

Hello!

And this is the immersion chamber that allows us to go out into the sea.

Oh! That's very interesting...

The air pressure is maintained inside the cupola by a series of pumps, which prevents the water from rising past a certain level, and a decompression chamber opens onto a small inner dock. But come...

Right behind you...

Here we are!

ARSENAL

The arsenal!

WALKING BEYOND THE HEAVY STEEL DOOR, THE TWO MEN ENTER A SERIES OF ROOMS WHERE WEAPONS AND AMMUNITION OF ALL TYPES AND CALIBRES ARE STACKED AS FAR AS THE EYE CAN SEE...

I say! You seem to be rather well stocked!

Yes, there's enough here for a nice little fireworks display...

And here, behind this concrete and steel wall, is the hydraulic press that compresses raw explosive materials, including our famous atomilite B.

A new type of explosive?

A single one of these sticks with a delayed contact detonator could reduce a ten-storey building to rubble!...

Good heavens! And...

BUT A CALL INTERRUPTS THE TWO MEN...

Hello!... Mallow! This is Captain Manderton. There's something fishy happening around the cyclotron... Take a look... And report to me as soon as possible.

MALLOW, WHO'S IMMEDIATELY TURNED ON HIS MICROPHONE, STEPS CLOSER TO A STEEL MOUNT FOR BETTER RECEPTION.

Very well, sir... We're going immediately.

AFTER RECEIVING THIS MESSAGE, MALLOW INTERRUPTS HIS PATROL AND HURRIEDLY LEAVES THE ARSENAL, FOLLOWED BY HARPER...

Come on, old fellow, we're needed!

Coming, coming!

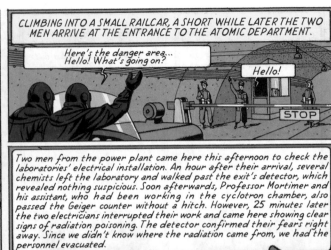

CLIMBING INTO A SMALL RAILCAR, A SHORT WHILE LATER THE TWO MEN ARRIVE AT THE ENTRANCE TO THE ATOMIC DEPARTMENT.

Here's the danger area... Hello! What's going on?

Hello!

STOP

Two men from the power plant came here this afternoon to check the laboratories' electrical installation. An hour after their arrival, several chemists left the laboratory and walked past the exit's detector, which revealed nothing suspicious. Soon afterwards, Professor Mortimer and his assistant, who had been working in the cyclotron chamber, also passed the Geiger counter without a hitch. However, 25 minutes later the two electricians interrupted their work and came here showing clear signs of radiation poisoning. The detector confirmed their fears right away. Since we didn't know where the radiation came from, we had the personnel evacuated.

Good. We'll go and have a look, then...

FOLLOWED BY HIS PARTNER, MALLOW RESOLUTELY STEPS INSIDE THE ATOMIC PLANT, HOLDING HIS GEIGER COUNTER BEFORE HIM...

Nothing suspicious here... This is the lead screen behind which all work takes place.

HAVING INSPECTED A SUCCESSION OF LABORATORIES WITHOUT FINDING ANYTHING OUT OF THE ORDINARY, THE TWO C.C....

By the way, isn't our friend Bell a specialist in nuclear matters?

Yes. And just between you and me, I wouldn't want to be in his place.

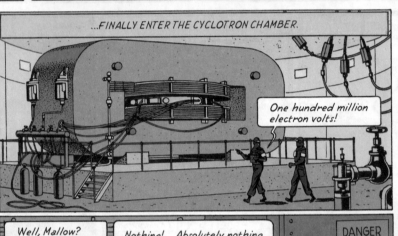

...FINALLY ENTER THE CYCLOTRON CHAMBER.

One hundred million electron volts!

Well, Mallow?

Nothing!... Absolutely nothing anywhere. Incidentally, which laboratory were these men last working in?

DANGER

In Dr Brown's, I think. Wait a minute... I just remembered... They said they went to the changing room and found a short circuit that they set about repairing. It was while they were doing that that the first signs of radiation poisoning appeared... But this couldn't possibly have anything to do with what concerns us here...

The changing room, you say?... Let's see...

Where were they exactly?

Over there. See, their ladder is still there.

They were here. Therefore, in all logic, it must...

NO ADMITTANCE WITHOUT CHANGING SHOES

BUT AT THAT MOMENT THE DETECTOR'S AUDIO SIGNAL CUTS SHORT MALLOW'S REFLECTIONS...

By Jove!

NO ADMITTANCE WITHOUT CHANGING

TEEEE TEEE TEEE

THANKS TO THE INDICATIONS OF THE GEIGER COUNTER'S FLUORESCENT SCREEN, THE PATROLLER QUICKLY LOCATES THE RADIOACTIVE ZONE...

There must be something there, just across from the ladder.

But what?

MALLOW APPROACHES A LAB COAT HANGING FROM A PEG AND EXAMINES IT CLOSELY BEFORE SUDDENLY PLUNGING HIS HAND INTO ONE OF THE POCKETS...

What on earth are you looking for?...

Ah!

This, dear fellow! Pliers turned radioactive! After repeated contact with radioactive material, these pliers are now also emitting extremely dangerous gamma rays... All the more dangerous since no one would think of being wary of the changing room!

Well, I'll be...! That's Stone's coat – the professor's assistant... He must have slipped the pliers into his pocket without thinking and forgotten all about it...

Small causes, great effects! But do step aside, for safety's sake.

SEVERAL MOMENTS LATER, THE TWO MEN RESUME THEIR INTERRUPTED PATROL AND LEAVE THE ATOMIC SECTOR. MALLOW MAKES HIS REPORT TO CAPTAIN MANDERTON.

...No sir, there's no danger... The items were safely stored inside the lead cabinet of the laboratory... Understood, Captain.

But Mallow, if there's a cyclotron here ... that means there's uranium as well?

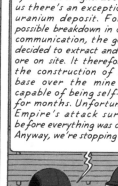

Well reasoned, old fellow! In fact, you could say there's a whole mine of it! That's right: 200 feet below us there's an exceptionally rich uranium deposit. Foreseeing a possible breakdown in our lines of communication, the government decided to extract and refine the ore on site. It therefore ordered the construction of a military base over the mine that was capable of being self-sufficient for months. Unfortunately, the Empire's attack surprised us before everything was completed... Anyway, we're stopping here.

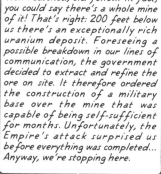

LEAVING THE RAILCAR, THE TWO C.C. START DOWN A LONG CORRIDOR...

Tell me, these openings I see everywhere... What are they for?

Air shafts... They come down from the ventilation room and connect several levels, and are themselves linked by other transverse air ducts. They contain steel ladders for inspections, and each patrol has a key opening the access grates... See...

Let me give you some light...

Hmm! Not a good place to be afraid of heights!...

Truly, Mallow, there's little chance of getting bored with you! But what's this?

The nerve centre of the base. Come in!

INSIDE A GREAT VAULTED HALL, SIX ENORMOUS TURBINE GENERATORS ARE HUMMING...

This is the plant that provides power for every sector of the base.

Fantastic! Although that doesn't tell me where the energy is coming from...

Patience... You'll soon see...

MALLOW LEADS HIS COMPANION ALONG A NARROW CORRIDOR DIVIDED BY MASSIVE AIRTIGHT HATCHES...

We're reaching the very heart of the base...

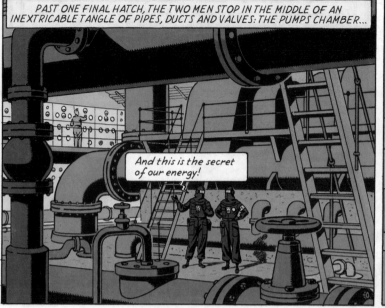

PAST ONE FINAL HATCH, THE TWO MEN STOP IN THE MIDDLE OF AN INEXTRICABLE TANGLE OF PIPES, DUCTS AND VALVES: THE PUMPS CHAMBER...

And this is the secret of our energy!

Through these huge pipes an unlimited, inexhaustible source of energy comes to us... The ocean's energy!

Goodness!

This process uses the temperature difference between surface waters and deep waters in tropical seas. It's very simple: the warm water from the surface comes to evaporate in the vacuum of a boiling chamber, and the resulting vapour condenses inside a condensation chamber when it comes into contact with cold water extracted from the deep. The vapour current created between the boiling chamber and the condensation chamber powers a large turbine, thereby converting thermal energy into mechanical energy, and finally into electrical energy by simply connecting the turbine to an alternator. And voilà!

Astounding!

This is really the vital point of the base, so now you understand the extraordinary security measures imposed on the personnel... One simple accident here or in the plant and we're paralysed...

Indeed I understand... No power, no Swordfish!...

Especially as time is running out! The Imperials suspect something, and it's now a real race between us...

Speaking of which, how close is that Swordfish to completion?

That?... You mean those Sw...Hey, you've dropped something...

I... Oh!?

A STICK OF ATOMILITE, ITS DETONATOR ALREADY SCREWED ON, HAS JUST FALLEN OUT OF HARPER'S POCKET.

Eh?!... What is this?... Atomilite!... But that means... You!... Hello! Hel...

Don't be a fool, Mallow!

Hello! Hello! This is central room... Who's calling?... Must have been a mistake... I could have sworn...

MEANWHILE, SIR WILLIAM AND CAPTAIN BLAKE HAVE GONE TO THE MANUFACTURING WORKSHOP TO HAVE A WORD WITH PROFESSOR MORTIMER.

Good day, gentlemen. Welcome to the workshop!

Hello, Professor!

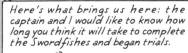

Here's what brings us here: the captain and I would like to know how long you think it will take to complete the Swordfishes and began trials.

Huh! You're catching me off guard... Obviously I don't intend to put your patience to the test, as I did with those gentlemen in Karachi... But why such a question?

So, sniffing around our door, are they?... In that case, gentlemen, I believe that within 20 days we could...

Well, numerous reports point towards the fact that Ras Musandam is currently under strangely intense scrutiny. All sorts of individuals are roaming the area: fake fishermen, fake merchants, refugees, etc.

Exactly as if the base had been found — or at least broadly located. I sent Nasir to the Makran side and am awaiting his return any moment now. If his report confirms our fears, very soon we'll have to make a decision on what response to offer...

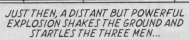

JUST THEN, A DISTANT BUT POWERFUL EXPLOSION SHAKES THE GROUND AND STARTLES THE THREE MEN...

BROOM

THEY HAVE BARELY SHAKEN OFF THE SURPRISE WHEN AN ALARMING MESSAGE REACHES THEM...

Hello! Hello! This is central room... Large explosion in the pumps chamber! Pumps five and six out of order!... Corridor three is under water!... Several injured!...

Good Lord!!!

Quick, let's go!

MOMENTS LATER, THE THREE MEN ARRIVE AT THE SITE OF THE ACCIDENT.

You see, gentlemen, everything was normal. The C.C. had just passed through on their patrol ... when ten minutes later a powerful explosion smashed pumps five and six. Water was gushing in with incredible force and filling the room with torrents of scalding vapour... I still managed to reach the control panel and shut off the intake valves. If the automatic emergency bulkheads hadn't closed, the whole chamber would have been flooded!

Has the C.C. patrol been seen again since, by the way?

No...

That's strange. We'd better warn the C.R.

Hello! Central room?... Is that you, Manderton?... Mortimer here.

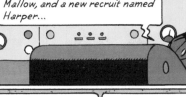

No, Professor. We've been trying to reach them for more than 15 minutes. I'm beginning to worry... Sorry?... Who?... Well, Mallow, and a new recruit named Harper...

Harper?...Heavens! Which way did they go?

I didn't really pay attention, but I think it was corridor three...

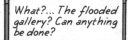

What?... The flooded gallery? Can anything be done?

Nothing for the moment, sir. The pumps are working, but we have to proceed carefully...

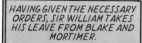

HAVING GIVEN THE NECESSARY ORDERS, SIR WILLIAM TAKES HIS LEAVE FROM BLAKE AND MORTIMER.

If there's any news about Harper I'll let you know immediately. As for you, notify me as soon as Nasir comes back.

Very well, sir.

Come on, old boy, snap out of it! And let's figure out how to deal with this new setback...

Yes, you're right Mortimer. It's just that I can't stop thinking about that poor chap... What a stupid accident...

Poor Harper! It's my fault...

Don't lose hope yet! They could be stuck inside a section that wasn't flooded...

Such are the hazards of war, Blake.

Ah, here's the technical section... Maybe we should take a look at Harper's room... He might have left some personal papers... It's unlikely but...

BLAKE WALKS UP TO THE DOOR AND KNOCKS...

Bell's in for a surprise.

HEARING NO ANSWER, HE OPENS THE DOOR AND ENTERS...

Forgive my intrusion, Bell, but...

Our man is a heavy sleeper, it seems...

SURPRISED, HE APPROACHES THE BED AND, SEIZED BY SUDDEN WORRY...

Hey! Bell! Bell!!... What on earth...? He...

...HE THROWS BACK THE COVERS. HARPER IS LYING THERE, UNCONSCIOUS, BELL'S BANDAGE AROUND HIS HEAD...

Good heavens!... But this is Harper!!!

A doctor... Quick!... And Sir William!

Right!

MOMENTS LATER, IN THE INFIRMARY...

Hello! Hello! The major is urgently needed in the technical section... Room 8!...

AS THEY WAIT FOR THE DOCTOR TO ARRIVE, BLAKE AND MORTIMER CONDUCT A QUICK EXAMINATION OF THE ROOM...

Yes, this is how it must have happened: Bell, a spy for the Imperials, sneaks into the prisoners' convoy, makes his way inside the base and, pretending to be indisposed, avoids the control committee. However, he knows he won't be able to do so for long. So, when Harper comes back with his C.C. uniform, Bell immediately sees its potential and decides to take his comrade's place. He hits Harper from behind, places him on the bed, wraps his head with his own bandage and heads to the C.R. Oh, if only we knew the face that was hiding behind that mysterious bandage and that rough beard!

Speaking of beard, someone here shaved in a hurry... Look: the soap dried on the brush and the razor wasn't cleaned... Moreover, the mess...

BUT THE DOOR OPENS BRUSQUELY...

Captain! Mallow's just been found at the bottom of an air shaft!

He's being brought back up now, but his injuries are severe...

Good Lord! Another one! Come on, Mortimer, let's go!

LYING ON A STRETCHER, THE UNFORTUNATE MALLOW IS BEING TAKEN TO THE INFIRMARY POST-HASTE.

Ah, there they are!

Can we question him, Doctor?

Yes, but hurry. He needs urgent care.

Mallow! Old fellow, can you tell me what happened?...

Ah! Captain...

WITH GREAT EFFORT, THE INJURED MAN MANAGES TO UTTER A FEW WORDS.

He... He stole ... atomilite from the arsenal... In corridor three... A stick fell out of his pocket... I... I tried to call ... but he... He... Ah!... Look out... Loo...

A SHORT WHILE LATER, GATHERED IN THE GOVERNOR'S OFFICE, THE THREE MEN DISCUSS THE EVENTS...

So that blasted spy is here somewhere, waiting for an opportunity to blow up some part of our base! Well, Blake, what do you propose?...

I see only one solution... As we do not have the manpower, we cannot afford to spread our forces. My idea is that...

BUT JUST THEN THE SPEAKER INTERRUPTS THE CAPTAIN...

Hello! Hello! This is guard station. The S2 is signalling his approach at periscope depth and requests the opening of the doors... It... Alert! Imperial aircraft in sight! Approaching rapidly from...

Alert!... Imperial squadron in sight! Anti-submarine aircraft, coming in fast... They must have spotted the periscope's wake... Yes, they have! Look out!!!

The devil! That's all we needed!!!

INDEED, TAKEN BY SURPRISE BY A LIGHTNING ATTACK, THE S2 IS SUDDENLY BRACKETED BY TORPEDOES AND DEPTH CHARGES.

THE SUBMARINE'S COMMANDER ORDERS AN EMERGENCY DIVE ... BUT THE CHARGES, DROPPED WITH DEADLY ACCURACY, EXPLODE EVER CLOSER...

...UNTIL...

BANG

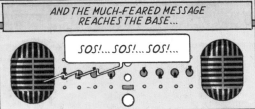

AND THE MUCH-FEARED MESSAGE REACHES THE BASE...

SOS!... SOS!... SOS!...

SOS!... Forward section damaged... Torpedo room flooded... Have reached sea bottom at 60 fathoms... 32 degrees list... Oxygen reserves: 6 hours... Awaiting instructions...

Gentlemen, things are happening fast ... but that doesn't mean we can forget about that spy! We're going to split the tasks: you, Blake, will take care of the man. You, Professor, the machines. As for me, I'll handle the S2. Understood?

All right.

Very well, sir.

Hello! Hello! This is Captain Blake. Control corps on alert!... To all patrols: your orders are to shoot on sight...

Hello!... The plant?... Is that you, Bill? Mortimer here. Listen carefully! We're expecting a sabotage attempt... Don't let anyone inside the room, do you hear? Absolutely no one... What was that? You already know?

AND MOMENTS LATER...

Hello! Hello! This is Governor William Gray! All divers on alert! Assemble the team in the immersion chamber... Full equipment...

Well, yes, Professor... A.C.C. just delivered your warning a second ago. He even insisted on checking himself that everything was... Sorry?... What!?... A spy!!!...

BUT AN UNUSUALLY POWERFUL BLAST CUTS THE CONVERSATION SHORT AND PLUNGES THE ENTIRE BASE INTO DARKNESS...

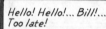
Hello! Hello!... Bill!... Too late!

Heavens! Would he dare? Hello! Hello! Atomic centre!...

THE PROFESSOR RUSHES OUT, BUT A FOREMAN RUNS TO HIM...

Professor, four of the turbines are gone!... The only ones left are the mine's and the workshop's!

Turn on the backup generators and connect the remaining turbines to the defence grid.

Good Lord! No answer!... But ... that would be a disaster!

I must warn them at all costs! Quick, my torch!...

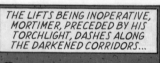
THE LIFTS BEING INOPERATIVE, MORTIMER, PRECEDED BY HIS TORCHLIGHT, DASHES ALONG THE DARKENED CORRIDORS...

May heaven grant that I arrive in time!

...AND AT LAST REACHES THE CHECKPOINT OF THE ATOMIC SECTOR.

Halt!

It's me, Mortimer!

Tell me, Lieutenant, has anyone tried to enter the sector? A.C.C., for example?... No?...

BUT AS HE STEPS INSIDE THE DESERTED PREMISES, MORTIMER IS INSTANTLY FILLED WITH FAINT APPREHENSION...

I should have brought my pistol...

No one, Professor. Actually, the sector was evacuated after the second explosion. Only Trenter stayed behind to guard the safe.

Phew! Thank goodness... Well, keep your eyes peeled!

PUSHING ASIDE THE STRANGE FEELING OF DREAD THAT HAS SEIZED HIM, MORTIMER HURRIES ON AND SOON REACHES THE RADIOCHEMICAL LAB. THE DOOR, LEFT AJAR, LETS OUT A THIN RAY OF YELLOW LIGHT. INSTINCTIVELY, THE PROFESSOR TURNS OFF HIS TORCH...

...BUT HE HASN'T TAKEN FIVE STEPS WHEN HE SUDDENLY STRIKES HIS FOOT AGAINST SOMETHING...

?

POINTING HIS TORCH AT THE OBSTACLE, MORTIMER CAN'T KEEP IN A STIFLED CRY: HIS ASSISTANT TRENTER IS LYING THERE, FACE DOWN AND UNCONSCIOUS...

Trenter!!!

BUT A FAINT NOISE COMING FROM THE LABORATORY STARTLES HIM.

But ... there's someone inside!

CREEPING CAREFULLY FORWARD, HE DISCOVERS, STANDING IN THE LIGHT OF A STORM LANTERN, A C.C. ATTEMPTING TO OPEN THE ARMOURED SAFE WHERE THE DANGEROUS RADIOACTIVE MATERIALS ARE KEPT.

Hell! If he opens that safe we're done for! I'm unarmed but there's no choice!

AND, RISKING IT ALL, MORTIMER SPRINGS FORWARD AND SEIZES THE MAN BY THE THROAT...

...BUT HIS OPPONENT, QUICK AS LIGHTNING, DUCKS AND MANAGES TO SQUIRM FREE, LEAVING HIS HOOD IN THE HANDS OF HIS ATTACKER. THE PROFESSOR, TAKEN ABACK...

...HAS NO TIME TO REACT. HIS FOE HAS TURNED ROUND TO FACE HIM, PISTOL IN HAND AND A THREATENING EXPRESSION ON HIS FACE...

Olrik!... You!... Here!...

Yes, the very same, my dear professor. My prestige was at stake and I refused to let another solve this problem... Oh, you had me well and truly fooled in Karachi, but the time to settle accounts is near, and I intend to pay back everything I owe you — with interest!

And now, hands in the air — and no monkey business, please... I'm no Dr Fo!... Go on, back... Good!

KEEPING HIS GUN TRAINED ON MORTIMER, OLRIK RETURNS TO OPENING THE SAFE.

I had run out of atomilite and was finding myself rather inconvenienced when I remembered that you kept something here that's much more ... effective!

AND NOW, PROFESSOR, HANDS IN THE AIR – AND NO MONKEY BUSINESS, PLEASE... I'M NO DR FO!!!

Salaam, Captain!

Hello, Nasir! What news?

...We've just found out that a traitor managed to sneak into the ranks of the C.C. That wretch has already blown up part of the power plant and is probably about to strike again... But go on, what else do you know?...

...According to the news from Karachi, Colonel Olrik hasn't been seen in three weeks...

What did you say?... Olrik's disappeared???...Good Lord! Could it be him?!... Tell me, what does he look like? Tall?

Sahib, Makran is full of troops, and the Imperials have found the trucks' hiding place. Moreover, many indications point towards the prisoner convoy being a mere ploy to infiltrate spies into the base...

I'll say! They can call it a resounding success!...

Yes, tall, dark, hawk-nosed... But sahib Mortimer would have recognised him, Captain...

No doubt, but as it happens the professor wasn't at the inspection that night... Well, I will get to the bottom of it...

Hello!... Is that you, old chap?... Ah!... And did the professor say where he was going?... To the atomic centre? Alone?... Fine....

If Olrik's here, we can expect the worst! Quick, Nasir, take this lamp and let's dash over there... Mortimer's absence worries me for some reason...

Yes, Captain.

IN THE MEANTIME, OLRIK HAS MANAGED TO OPEN THE LABORATORY'S SAFE AND...

Ah! This will do nicely!

...HAVING REMOVED A SERIES OF GLASS PHIALS CONTAINING RADIOACTIVE SUBSTANCES, IS ABOUT TO PUT HIS HOOD BACK ON WHEN...

Hey! But...

...how about we settle our scores first ... eh?... What do you think, my dear professor?

Personally, I think such a question is premature, Colonel! Hands up!!!

?

By Jove, Blake, that's what I call arriving in the nick of time! A minute later and our friend would have sent me to meet my ancestors!

The game is up, Olrik!... Drop your weapon! Nasir, go and tie up his hands...

Curses!!!

AS NASIR ADVANCES TOWARDS HIM, ROPE IN HAND, OLRIK SEEMS MOMENTARILY CRUSHED BY THE SUDDEN REVERSAL OF FORTUNE...

Your turn now, dear fellow!

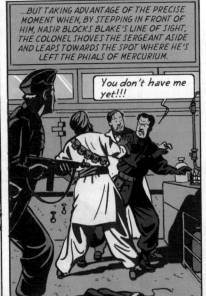

...BUT TAKING ADVANTAGE OF THE PRECISE MOMENT WHEN, BY STEPPING IN FRONT OF HIM, NASIR BLOCKS BLAKE'S LINE OF SIGHT, THE COLONEL SHOVES THE SERGEANT ASIDE AND LEAPS TOWARDS THE SPOT WHERE HE'S LEFT THE PHIALS OF MERCURIUM.

You don't have me yet!!!

HAVING GRABBED ONE OF THEM, HE FACES HIS OPPONENTS, FULL OF RESOLVE.

If any of you takes a single step forward, I will crush this phial!... And you know what that would mean!!!...

OLRIK, ARM RAISED AND READY TO SMASH THE FRAGILE GLASS CONTAINER, MOVES FORWARD THREATENINGLY...

Put down that sub-machine gun!... Go on, step back, all of you!... Clear the door!!!

FULLY AWARE OF THE DRAMATIC CONSEQUENCES THAT WOULD FOLLOW IF SUCH A THREAT WAS CARRIED OUT, THE THREE MEN COMPLY...

STILL BRANDISHING HIS DIABOLICAL INSTRUMENT, OLRIK REACHES THE DOOR AND PREPARES TO STEP ACROSS THE THRESHOLD WHEN...

...CHANGING HIS MIND, WITH AN ANGRY GESTURE HE THROWS THE PHIAL TOWARDS THE GROUP.

THE DEADLY PROJECTILE PASSES MERE INCHES ABOVE THE HEAD OF MORTIMER, WHO BARELY HAS TIME TO DUCK, AND...

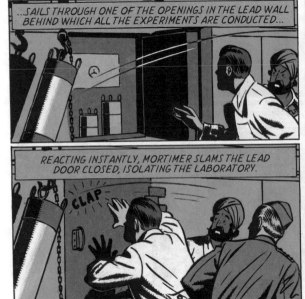

...SAILS THROUGH ONE OF THE OPENINGS IN THE LEAD WALL BEHIND WHICH ALL THE EXPERIMENTS ARE CONDUCTED...

REACTING INSTANTLY, MORTIMER SLAMS THE LEAD DOOR CLOSED, ISOLATING THE LABORATORY.

CLAP

JUST THEN, THE POWER COMES BACK ON, FLOODING THE ROOM WITH STARK ELECTRIC LIGHT...

...BUT OLRIK, SEEING THE FAILURE OF HIS ATTACK AND HIS ENEMIES READY TO RUSH AT HIM, QUICKLY CLOSES THE DOOR...

...AND LOCKS IT FROM THE OUTSIDE.

Oh, he won't go very far now that the light's back. Speaking of which...

Too late!!!

Hello! Hello! Guard station?... This is Blake... We're locked inside the lab... Yes, that's right... But watch out — a man wearing a C.C. uniform is going to attempt to leave this sector. Have every exit patrolled and at the first sign of resistance open fire!

Sergeant! Alert every available man... The spy is in this sector!... Three men with me – I'm heading to the laboratory. Quickly!

Very good, sir!

No, sir, we didn't see anyone on our way here...

He can't possibly have left the atomic sector – every exit is guarded... Search everything room by room!

...The rogue must surely be hiding in some corner. So, here's what we're going to do: you Mortimer, you'll take care of the lab – check and, if possible, neutralise the radioactive effects of the broken phial. I'll have some help sent to you. As for Nasir and me, we'll join the search parties...

All right! But watch yourselves. If he's cornered, that fellow is capable of anything ... as I'm all too aware of!

IN SMALL GROUPS, FINGERS ON TRIGGERS, SOLDIERS CARRY OUT THE INSPECTION OF THE DESERTED ATOMIC SECTOR...

Keep your eyes peeled, boys!

HOWEVER, OLRIK DIDN'T WAIT FOR HIS OPPONENTS TO FIND HIM. HAVING OPENED THE GRATE OF AN AIR VENT, HE SWIFTLY SLIPS INSIDE AND, STEPPING ONTO THE STEEL LADDER, BEGINS CLIMBING...

I suppose I'll see where this takes me...

Isn't this ever going to end?...

BUT THE AIR SHAFTS, INTERCONNECTED BY A WHOLE NETWORK OF GALLERIES, FORM A VERITABLE MAZE, AND OLRIK IS BEGINNING TO THINK HE'S LOST WHEN...

...ALL AT ONCE, AROUND A CORNER OF THE CORRIDOR, HE SEES A GLIMMER OF LIGHT FILTERING THROUGH AN AIR VENT...

Ah!

...AND, HAVING APPROACHED SOUNDLESSLY, HE CASTS A CAUTIOUS GLANCE THROUGH THE GRATE COVERING THE OPENING...

The diving suits room!

IT IS INDEED THE DIVING SUITS CHANGING ROOM, AND A MAN IS CURRENTLY BUSY DONNING HIS UNDERWATER EQUIPMENT, CURSING THE WHILE.

Hell's bells! I need to hurry! That damned buckle has delayed me...

MEANWHILE, IN THE ATOMIC SECTOR, THE SEARCH CONTINUES IN VAIN AND BLAKE IS BEGINNING TO LOSE PATIENCE...

Blast it!... He can't have just vanished!!!

SUDDENLY A SOFT GRATING SOUND CATCHES NASIR'S ATTENTION...

CRRRSS

Hell! The air shaft!... I hadn't thought of that... Of course, the C.C. have the key...

Sahib! Look! The grate is opened!

Quickly! Go and warn the lieutenant! Bring him back with half a dozen men. I'll wait here...

Yes, sahib!

BUT, LEFT ALONE, BLAKE CANNOT RESIST THE URGE TO PURSUE THE FUGITIVE.

Every minute counts!... Oh, hang it! They'll catch me up.

AT THAT MOMENT, A PETTY OFFICER DASHES INTO THE CHANGING ROOM...

Oi, O'Connell!! We're all waiting on you!

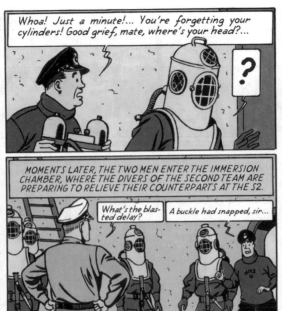

Whoa! Just a minute!... You're forgetting your cylinders! Good grief, mate, where's your head?...

?

MOMENTS LATER, THE TWO MEN ENTER THE IMMERSION CHAMBER, WHERE THE DIVERS OF THE SECOND TEAM ARE PREPARING TO RELIEVE THEIR COUNTERPARTS AT THE S2.

What's the blasted delay?

A buckle had snapped, sir...

AFTER A QUICK INSPECTION OF THE EQUIPMENT, THE HATCH IS OPENED AND THE MEN SLOWLY MAKE THEIR WAY INTO THE DECOMPRESSION CHAMBER.

Inside, boys!

A LITTLE LATER...

All right, open the door to the well...

Pressure normalised, sir.

MEANWHILE, BLAKE, HAVING FOLLOWED OLRIK'S FOOTPRINTS IN THE DUST, ARRIVES AT THE CHANGING ROOM'S AIR VENT...

Ah, there's light!... Better approach carefully...

The grate is unlocked... So this is the place.

No one!... And yet he must have exited here, there's no doubt... But then what? Ah! Let's look at the dormitory. Perhaps...

BLAKE TAKES A STEP TOWARDS THE EXIT BUT HIS FOOT BECOMES CAUGHT IN A STRAP TRAILING ON THE FLOOR...

?

AND THE STRAP TURNS OUT TO BE THE NECK LOOP OF A C.C. COMMUNICATION DEVICE.

A walkie-talkie!!! Then... Ah, what's under this bench? Let's see...

BLAKE HAS NOTICED A SORT OF BUNDLE COVERED BY A BLANKET. LIFTING A CORNER HE CANNOT HOLD BACK A STARTLED CRY: A MAN IS LYING THERE!

Good heavens!

IN THE MEANTIME, THE DIVERS HAVE ENTERED THE IMMERSION CUPOLA. TURNING THEIR HEADLAMPS ON, THEY LOWER THEMSELVES INTO THE WELL THAT LEADS TO THE UNDERWATER GALLERY CONNECTED TO THE SEA.

BLAKE, DASHING OUT OF THE CHANGING ROOM, TURNS TO THE NEAREST MAN...

Are there any divers leaving right now?

Aye, sir... The second team is assembling in the immersion chamber.

...BEFORE RUNNING INTO THE IMMERSION CHAMBER...

Chief, where are the men of the second team?

Er... Gone, sir!

AT THAT PRECISE MOMENT, THE DIVERS COME OUT OF THE GALLERY AND INTO THE SEA PROPER...

IN A FEW WORDS BLAKE EXPLAINS THE SITUATION TO THE DIVING CHIEF.

Travelling through the air shafts, the spy reached the changing room, surprised and knocked out the man getting suited up ... and took his place among the outgoing team!

Blimey! That's bold!!!

Right, there's not a moment to lose... Quick, a suit and an 'aquatic gun'.

Straight away, sir!

TIME IS INDEED OF THE ESSENCE, AS OLRIK, WHO MADE SURE HE BROUGHT UP THE REAR, HAS HUNG BACK DISCREETLY AND, LEAVING HIS COMPANIONS TO CONTINUE ON THEIR WAY TO THE S2, IMMEDIATELY CHANGES DIRECTION TO START CLIMBING THE SLOPE LEADING TO THE SHORE...

BLAKE, NOW GEARED UP, IS PREPARING TO GO THROUGH THE AIRLOCK AS NASIR, WHO'S FINALLY CAUGHT UP WITH HIM, TRIES IN VAIN TO CONVINCE HIM TO WAIT FOR AN ESCORT.

Impossible – he already has too much of a lead on us. Warn Sir William and the professor.

As you wish, sahib. And may Allah protect you!

SOON AFTER, BLAKE TOO EXITS THE BASE AND REACHES THE SEA...

No point in looking towards the S2. He's more likely to try and reach the surface by walking along the ocean floor. Forward!

THE CAPTAIN CLIMBS THE UNEVEN SLOPE AND, REACHING A KIND OF PROMONTORY, SWITCHES OFF HIS HEADLAMP AND BEGINS TO SCAN HIS DARK SURROUNDINGS.

He's bound to have to turn on his light any second now...

SUDDENLY, MAYBE THREE CABLE LENGTHS FROM HIM, A LIGHT SHOOTS OUT FROM A DIP IN THE TERRAIN!...THEN THE BEAM, SHAKING FRANTICALLY, BEGINS SWEEPING ACROSS THE SURROUNDING ROCKS IN HAPHAZARD FASHION...

Is he signalling someone?...

NONPLUSSED BUT INTRIGUED, BLAKE HURRIES DOWN FROM HIS VANTAGE POINT AND APPROACHES THE HOLLOW, PISTOL IN HAND... ONLY TO BE STUNNED BY THE HORROR OF THE SIGHT HE DISCOVERS.

BEFORE HIM, IN A ROCKY DEPRESSION, OLRIK, KNIFE IN HAND, IS FIGHTING FOR HIS LIFE AGAINST A GIGANTIC OCTOPUS IN A HIDEOUS TANGLE OF TENTACLES.

WITHOUT HESITATION, BLAKE LEAPS INTO THE FRAY AND, AIMING AT ONE OF THE ENORMOUS GLASSY EYES, RIDDLES THE MONSTER WITH BULLETS FROM HIS 'AQUATIC GUN'.

THE CEPHALOPOD, DOUBTLESS SUFFERING DAMAGE TO A VITAL ORGAN, IMMEDIATELY RELEASES ITS GRIP AND JETS AWAY IN A GREAT CLOUD OF INK.

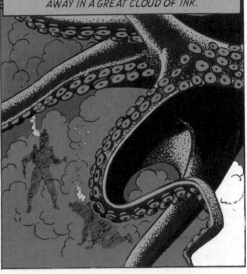

FEARING A NEW TREACHERY, BLAKE ADVANCES TOWARDS OLRIK. BUT THE COLONEL, SPRAWLED ON THE SAND AND EXHAUSTED, DROPS HIS KNIFE AND SIGNALS HIS SURRENDER...

MEANWHILE, BACK AT BASE, A WORRIED MORTIMER IS PREPARING TO GO AND LOOK FOR HIS FRIEND WITH A FEW MEN.

Leaving alone – how reckless!!!

NEVERTHELESS, BLAKE AND HIS PRISONER ARE SLOWLY MAKING THEIR WAY BACK...

BUT WHILE CROSSING A JUMBLE OF ROCKS AND SEASHELLS, THE CAPTAIN FEELS HIS LEG ABRUPTLY CAUGHT IN A VICE... AN ENORMOUS BIVALVE HAS JUST CLOSED AROUND HIS FOOT...

LOSING HIS BALANCE AND FALLING DOWN, BLAKE ATTEMPTS TO SHOOT THE MOLLUSC THROUGH THE GAP IN THE SHELL, BUT IS DISMAYED TO DISCOVER THAT HIS WEAPON IS EMPTY!

OLRIK, NOT SEEING THE LIGHT FROM BLAKE'S HEADLAMP ANY MORE, TURNS ROUND. SPOTTING THE BRITON ON THE GROUND...

...HE IMMEDIATELY RETRACES HIS STEPS AND WALKS TOWARDS HIS IMMOBILISED OPPONENT, SNEERING...

Ha! Ha! You look somewhat trapped, my dear captain!

...AND, SEIZING THE AIR HOSE, ATTEMPTS TO PULL IT OUT. THE UNFORTUNATE BLAKE, HIS LEG CRUSHED BY THE BIVALVE, DESPERATELY ATTEMPTS TO FEND HIM OFF...

HAMPERED BY HIS ENEMY'S RESISTANCE, OLRIK NONETHELESS SUCCEEDS IN BENDING THE AIR INTAKE OF THE BREATHING APPARATUS, AND BLAKE ALREADY BEGINS TO WEAKEN. BUT THE ROGUE SUDDENLY BREAKS OFF HIS SINISTER WORK... SEVERAL LIGHTS HAVE APPEARED NEARBY...

Curses! They're coming!... I must run...

INDEED, MORTIMER AND HIS MEN, ADVANCING TOWARDS THE COAST, HAVE JUST SEEN THE BEAMS OF THE HEADLAMPS.

There!

ABANDONING HIS SUFFOCATING VICTIM, OLRIK SMASHES BLAKE'S LAMP, TURNS OFF HIS OWN AND WITHOUT LINGERING ANY LONGER TAKES FLIGHT...

BUT THE RESCUERS HAVE RUSHED FORWARD, 'AQUATIC GUNS' IN HAND. SPRINTING THROUGH THE OBSTACLES STREWN ALONG THEIR PATH...

...THEY ARRIVE AT THE SCENE OF THE TRAGEDY, WHERE BLAKE LIES UNCONSCIOUS...

Lord!!!

IMMEDIATELY COMING TO THE POOR FELLOW'S HELP, THE DIVERS SOON HAVE HIS LEG FREE AND HIS BREATHING APPARATUS REPAIRED. REALISING THE FUTILITY OF A HAZARDOUS CHASE...

...MORTIMER ORDERS THE GROUP TO RETURN TO THE BASE AS QUICKLY AS POSSIBLE...

We shall meet again!...

Ah! A fisherman's hut!...

WHILE THESE DRAMATIC EVENTS UNFOLD, 60 FATHOMS BELOW THE SURFACE, NEARBY ON THE COAST, A MAN IS TRAVELLING AT HIS MOUNT'S SLOW PACE. IT'S OUR OLD ACQUAINTANCE THE BEZENDJAS, ON A SURVEILLANCE MISSION.

Salaam be with you, fisherman... Can you give me hospitality for the night?

You are welcome in my humble home, Bezendjas.

AS NIGHT FALLS, THE TWO MEN SHARE A HOOKAH AND CHAT AROUND THE FIRE...

So, are you happy with the life you live in this isolated place?

Fish is plentiful and the area quiet. And yet the new moon will no longer find me here...

Oh? And why is that? Does the noise from the patrol aircraft frighten you so much?...

No, I'm leaving because these waters are haunted... Sometimes you can see strange lights in the sea...

...This very afternoon, there were terrifying rumbles coming from the depths. The earth shook and over there, around that solitary rock, I saw the waters bubble and froth...

Well, well...

IN THE MEANTIME, BLAKE WAS BROUGHT BACK TO THE BASE AND RECEIVED INTENSIVE CARE FROM THE MEDICAL OFFICER. REVIVED, HE NOW TAKES PART IN THE GENERAL STAFF MEETING PRESIDED OVER BY SIR WILLIAM...

...It's quite obvious that Olrik is going to bring the Imperials back here – in force...

There's no doubt about it! Which means that since the S2's crew are now safe, we can focus all our attention on the base...

...Let's examine our strategic situation first. To the east, the Gulf of Oman. To the west, the Persian Gulf... But the loss of our last submarine rules out all attempts at even partial evacuation on those sides... To the south, well, for one thing the coast is closely guarded, and then there's the ad-Dahna ... 800 miles across red sand desert! An impassable obstacle in the current circumstances! Finally, to the north, the Strait of Hormuz and Makran. But we can forget about using the tunnel too. Olrik knows where the entrance is and his first order of business will be to set up an ambush there. Therefore, gentlemen, there's only one alternative: we put all our defences on full alert immediately. The question will be whether we'll be able to count on support from the Swordfishes!... Thank heavens that cursed spy didn't reach the workshops....

No, but he still managed to reduce our power to a quarter of its maximum output!...

So?...

As you know, the Swordfish was designed to be equipped with a robotic pilot. A whole squadron is already on the assembly line ready to receive that device. Unfortunately, its final development – slow, painstaking work – is far from being done. So here's what I propose: we replace the remote-control equipment with a conventional cockpit and turn all our efforts towards completing the first two Swordfishes. They will have the dangerous task of meeting and blunting the enemy attack. In the meantime, we will finish the other aircraft and throw them into the fray as they are completed. However, I must warn you that this is terribly risky and that it is impossible to foresee what awaits the first man who pilots such a machine!...

It's a risk we'll have to take, as we have no choice... Sir, I'm ready to fly the first Swordfish.

And I the second one.

Jolly good, gentlemen! I expected no less from you... And how long do you estimate you'll need to get the first aircraft in fighting order?

Barring the unexpected, a minimum of 30 hours ... assuming we hold that long!

We'll hold!... It is now midnight. The day after tomorrow, at 6.00 a.m., the first two Swordfishes will go into action. It will be the end or the beginning!... Get to work, Professor, and good luck! Blake, you get the base to action stations... Gentlemen, the world's freedom depends on us!

You can count on us, sir!

Hello! Hello! All sectors! Red alert!... All hands to action stations!... Man the security systems!... Hello! Hello!... Red alert!...

AS THAT IMPORTANT CONFERENCE DRAWS TO A CLOSE THE BEZENDJAS, INTRIGUED BY THE PERPLEXING WORDS OF THE FISHERMAN, CONVINCES THE LOCAL TO ACCOMPANY HIM TO THE SHORE.

So that's the rock, eh?...

BUT SUDDENLY OVER THE CRASH OF THE WAVES COMES A LONG MOAN, RISING THEN FALLING ABRUPTLY.

May Allah protect us! A ghost!!!

Quiet, you old fool!... That was someone calling out...

ABANDONING HIS FEARFUL COMPANION, THE BEZENDJAS, LEAPING FROM ROCK TO ROCK, HURRIES TOWARDS THE SPOT WHERE THE MOAN CAME FROM.

A diver!...

Beware!

THE BEZENDJAS LEANS OVER THE MAN AND IS ASTONISHED TO RECOGNISE, THROUGH THE HELMET'S SMASHED PORTHOLE, THE MOONLIT FACE OF HIS MASTER, COLONEL OLRIK...

The colonel!!!!

A FEW HOURS LATER...

THE BASE IS FILLED WITH FRANTIC ACTIVITY...

Remove that panel too... We have to clear the forward section as much as possible to maximise visibility.

Understood, Professor.

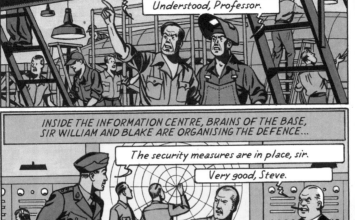

INSIDE THE INFORMATION CENTRE, BRAINS OF THE BASE, SIR WILLIAM AND BLAKE ARE ORGANISING THE DEFENCE...

The security measures are in place, sir.

Very good, Steve.

AND IN THE FISHERMAN'S HUT, WHERE OLRIK WAS TAKEN, THE BEZENDJAS ANXIOUSLY SCANS THE COLONEL'S FACE AFTER HOURS SPENT TRYING TO ROUSE HIM FROM UNCONSCIOUSNESS. SUDDENLY THE RENEGADE LETS OUT A LONG SIGH AND OPENS HIS EYES.

A last!!! Allah be praised!

How are you feeling, sahib? It's me, Razul, your loyal servant...

Ah, the Bezendjas! How did I get here?

WHILE THE BEZENDJAS BRIEFLY RELATES THE CIRCUMSTANCES THAT LED HIM TO FIND THE UNCONSCIOUS BODY OF HIS MASTER, THE COLONEL ATTEMPTS TO PIECE TOGETHER HIS RECOLLECTIONS...

...When I saw the broken porthole I was worried, sahib...

...I must have moved off course and I wandered in the darkness for a long time... I'd almost lost hope when I finally reached the surface, but my air was running out... I fell on a rock and when the porthole was smashed, it let the air in... But...

But... Dammit! How long was I unconscious?

Four hours, sahib!

The devil! They're going to escape!... How far is the nearest outpost?

Ninety miles away, sahib...

All right. You're going to head there this minute with a message for the commanding officer and the order to telegraph it to Karachi... The base is ours!... We must alert all available forces!... I'll wait here ... but by all the demons of hell, make haste!

Count on me, sahib.

FIFTEEN MINUTES LATER, AS THE SKY BEGINS TO TURN LIGHT IN THE EAST, THE BEZENDJAS RIDES AWAY AT A FAST TROT, CARRYING THE MESSAGE.

THE SUN HAS RISEN AND THE HOURS GO BY, TOO SLOWLY FOR OLRIK'S LIKING. FULLY RECOVERED, HE CANNOT CONTAIN HIS IMPATIENCE.

What are they doing?... He's been gone for more than ten hours!...

BUT THE TENSION IS EQUALLY HIGH AMONG HIS OPPONENTS; AIR AND SURFACE RADARS ROTATE CEASELESSLY FROM THE TOP OF THE ROCK, AND ULTRASONIC DETECTORS LISTEN TO EVERY SOUND IN THE DEPTHS...

ALL AT ONCE THE OPERATOR ON DUTY NOTICES THE APPEARANCE OF A TINY V-SHAPED BREAK IN THE BRIGHT LINE OF THE AIR DEFENCE RADAR'S SCREEN...

Hello! Hello!... Planes detected 98 miles north-east of the base!

37

NEWS OF THE APPROACH OF ENEMY SQUADRONS HAS BARELY REACHED THE INFORMATION CENTRE BEFORE OTHER MESSAGES FOLLOW IN QUICK AND OMINOUS SUCCESSION FROM THE OTHER WATCH POSTS...

Hello! Hello! This is surface watch. Contacts detected at 50 miles south, south-east. Probably three large ships and ten destroyers. Another contact comprising a heavy unit and five smaller vessels 43 miles to the west, south-west.

They must be coming from Muscat...

And the others from Bahrain...

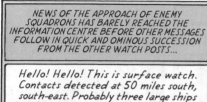

Hello! Hello! This is underwater watch. ASDIC reports a dozen submarines at least 34 miles to the south-east, and 3 or 4 west, north-west, at 39 miles.

Hello! Hello! This is aerial watch. Large formation 35 miles to the east, south-east... It seems to be splitting into 2 groups... One of them is turning straight to the north, north-west...

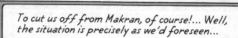

To cut us off from Makran, of course!... Well, the situation is precisely as we'd foreseen...

Absolutely, sir... Which is why I'm going to make one last inspection...

INDEED, A FEW MINUTES LATER AN IMPRESSIVE FORMATION OF FOUR-ENGINED AIRCRAFT TOWING TROOP-LADEN GLIDERS APPEARS ON THE HORIZON.

THE GLIDERS LAND ON THE BEACH ONE AFTER THE OTHER... OLRIK, WHO HAS RUSHED TO MEET THE NEWCOMERS...

...IMMEDIATELY MAKES CONTACT WITH THE COMMANDER OF THE AIRBORNE TROOPS.

Colonel, by special order of His Majesty, all available units have been sent to you and placed under your direct command...

I am deeply honoured, General, and, believe me, the Emperor will have no cause to regret the trust he has placed in me... We have them this time!!!

WHILE ON THE SHORE THE AIRBORNE TROOPS RAPIDLY TAKE UP POSITIONS IN FRONT OF THE BASE...

...OLRIK EXPLAINS HIS PLAN OF ATTACK TO THE OFFICERS OF HIS STAFF.

So it's that rock over there that we have to take? Hmm! It won't be easy, I'm afraid!

Certainly, the operation will be costly. But the stakes are high enough to justify the losses. Just think... The lair of the Swordfish!!!

...But look at the map, gentlemen!... Here, at the centre of our deployment, is the base: that isolated rock a good half-mile out to sea... To the south, deployed along the coast, our artillery is pointed at it. On the other side of the strait is the tunnel's exit, currently guarded by our 2nd Airborne Group... Finally, to the east and west, our fleet and carrier-based squadrons... We might as well say that the base is at our mercy. As soon as the navy is in position as per the attack plan, we will spring into action.

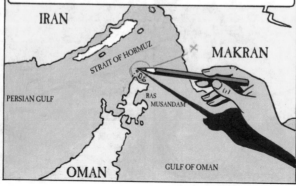

IRAN

MAKRAN

STRAIT OF HORMUZ

PERSIAN GULF

RAS MUSANDAM

OMAN

GULF OF OMAN

But why risk a frontal attack in open terrain instead of waiting for the 2nd Airborne to enter the tunnel?

Because that group will be delayed by tremendous obstacles: quicksands, armoured doors and narrow passages to be blasted open, etc. And because every hour that passes might cost us the fruit of our efforts: the secret of the Swordfish!... And now, gentlemen, please excuse me while I don a uniform worthy of my rank.

TWO HOURS LATER, BLAKE, HAVING COMPLETED HIS LAST-MINUTE INSPECTION, REPORTS TO GOVERNOR SIR WILLIAM GRAY.	...Down in the magazines, whose stockpiles will let us hold for several weeks, ammunition is ready to be hoisted up...	...to the gun emplacements, where the artillery waits only for the word to remove the camouflaged portholes and open fire.	Every embrasure is bristling with machine guns, flame-throwers, bazookas...	...and we don't have to fear an underwater assault, as our minefield is all but impassable.

...I checked the entire system and I'm now in the lookout post... Morale is excellent at every level and the men are calm and resolute as they wait for the clash...

    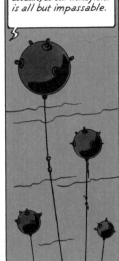

Finally, regarding the Makran sector, the tunnel is fully locked up. The portcullises and doors are closed and plan B is ready to come into play... According to the latest news, the Imperials are crossing the quicksands with heavy...

What's that?... The Imperial fleet is in sight?... I'm on my way!...

AND MOMENTS LATER...

Smoke in sight, bearing 262!!!

And there are the others!... Perfect!

BUT A LOOKOUT'S CRY INTERRUPTS THE COMMUNICATION...

Captain! Smoke! Bearing 98 degrees!

That's right... An aircraft carrier... Two cruisers and seven ... eight ... nine destroyers!

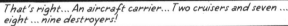

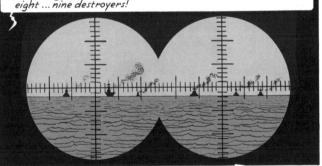

The artillery on the coast seems about to open fire!!!

Hello! Hello! This is the information centre... The Makran watch post reports that the enemy is now in front of door number one!

Well!... Shut off the radars and clear the embrasures!... Blake, tell Mortimer and then patch me through to the general circuit. I'd like to say a few words to the men before it starts...

Yes, sir.

Hello! Mortimer, the party's about to kick off!... We'll do the impossible to hold long enough... As for you, do your best...

All right!... You can count on us, old chap. And in the meantime make them dance!!!

Boys, the time for action has come!... Your comrades in the assembly room are currently finishing...

AT THAT MOMENT, A RED FLARE, FIRED FROM THE LINES OF THE ATTACKERS, LAUNCHES INTO THE SKY AND BURSTS! THE IMPERIALS ARE ATTACKING!!!

...the weapon that will enable us to take our revenge and recover our freedom... Professor Mortimer asked for a 30-hour delay... I promised he would have it, knowing that you wouldn't make a liar out of me: 'England expects that every man will do his duty!!!'

Hurrah! Hurrah! Hurrah! Hurrah!

AT THE SIGNAL, THE SHIPS, WHICH HAVE CLOSED TO LESS THAN THREE MILES FROM THEIR TARGET, OPEN FIRE WITH THEIR HEAVY BATTERIES...

...IMMEDIATELY FOLLOWED BY THE GROUND-BASED ARTILLERY, THE MULTIPLE ROCKET-LAUNCHERS DISGORGING THEIR DEADLY CARGO.

AND WHILE FIGHTERS AND BOMBERS TAKE OFF FROM THE AIRCRAFT CARRIER AND BEAR DOWN AT THE ROCK LIKE A FLOCK OF VULTURES...

...THE SUBMARINES, TORPEDOES AND LIMPET MINES AT THE READY, GLIDE SILENTLY TOWARDS THE BASE'S MAIN GATE...

ASSAILED FROM ALL DIRECTIONS, THE ROCK DISAPPEARS UNDER A HAIL OF BOMBS, ROCKETS AND SHELLS, AND IS SOON TURNED INTO A RAGING INFERNO...

STANDING READY BEHIND THEIR GUNS, THE DEFENDERS WAIT... WHEN SUDDENLY...

Oh heck! Smoke shells!!!

AT LAST, AFTER 30 MINUTES OF CONSTANT SHELLING, THE BARRAGE STOPS AS QUICKLY AS IT HAD BEGUN...

That's enough for now. Send in the assault barges...

PROTECTED BY THE SMOKE SCREEN AND SUPPORTED BY THE DESTROYERS, THE ASSAULT BARGES, CRAMMED WITH MEN AND LOW ON THE WATER, RUSH FORWARD.

HIS EYES GLUED TO THE BINOCULARS, SIR WILLIAM VAINLY TRIES TO SEE THROUGH THE ARTIFICIAL FOG.

Dammit! Can't make out a thing through that blasted fog!

Hello! Hello! This is the information centre... Makran watch reports the Imperials are through door number one. They are inside the cave and advancing towards the bridge!!!

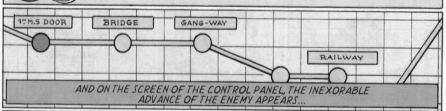

1ᵀᴴ M.S DOOR | BRIDGE | GANG-WAY | RAILWAY

AND ON THE SCREEN OF THE CONTROL PANEL, THE INEXORABLE ADVANCE OF THE ENEMY APPEARS...

Right!... C.P. to Makran watch... Ready on plan B... C.P. to artillery. All batteries standing by?... Good...

If only the wind could pick up... Ah! There they are!... Two cable lengths away!... Ready, Blake?...

Fire!...

EVERY GUN IN THE BASE OPENS UP AT ONCE. STRUCK AT POINT-BLANK RANGE, THE BARGES SINK WITH ALL HANDS WHILE SEVERAL DESTROYERS THAT HAD CARELESSLY MOVED TOO CLOSE HASTILY RETREAT WITH SEVERE DAMAGE...

LURED IN BY THE ABSENCE OF AERIAL RESISTANCE, LOW-FLYING PLANES ARE PROMPTLY TARGETED BY THE ANTI-AIRCRAFT DEFENCE'S MAGNETIC ROCKETS...

...WHILE BELOW THE SURFACE THE SUBMARINES RUN FOUL OF THE MINEFIELDS THAT PROTECT THE APPROACHES TO THE MAIN ENTRANCE...

THE TERRIFIC DAMAGE INFLICTED BY THE FIERCENESS AND SUDDENNESS OF THE DEFENCE STOPS THE IMPERIAL ASSAULT DEAD IN ITS TRACKS...

Look at this with a calm mind, gentlemen! And remember that by keeping the British's attention on this sector, we are making things much easier for the troops that are currently progressing through the tunnel.

But... But our losses are enormous, Colonel!

INDEED, WHILE THE BATTLE RAGES ON ABOVE THE WAVES, THE IMPERIALS HAVE SUCCEEDED IN BREACHING THE FIRST DOOR AND ARE NOW PREPARING TO CROSS THE BRIDGE THAT SPANS THE CRAB PIT...

BUT THE OFFICER WHO LEADS THE COLUMN, UNKNOWINGLY CUTTING THE INVISIBLE BEAM OF A CAESIUM ELECTRIC EYE, TRIGGERS THE RELEASE OF PLAN B, WHICH THE MAKRAN WATCH POST HAS JUST PRECISELY EXECUTED. AND...

1ST MS DOOR · BRIDGE · GANG-WAY · RAILW

...WITH A BLINDING FLASH OF LIGHT FOLLOWED BY A SHOCKING EXPLOSION, THE BRIDGE'S SPAN IS BLOWN TO PIECES, CASTING THE IMPERIALS INTO THE ABYSS. AND AS DEBRIS RAINS DOWN AND CRUSHES EVERYTHING UNDERNEATH, THE DEFLAGRATION'S VAST POWER SHATTERS WHOLE SECTIONS OF WALLS...

...THAT COLLAPSE ON THE SURVIVORS WHO'D RETREATED TO THE TUNNELS IN COMPLETE DISARRAY.

HEARING NEWS OF THE DISASTER, A SEETHING OLRIK ORDERS A GENERAL RETREAT, AND SOON...

Hello! Hello! This is the information centre! The Imperials are falling back everywhere!...

Boys!... The score's one-nil for old England!

Outstanding!... But watch out for the second half!

ABOARD THE CARRIER WHERE OLRIK HAS TRANSFERRED HIS COMMAND POST, THE MOOD IS TENSE. INFURIATED BY THEIR FAILURE, THE IMPERIAL OFFICERS ARE CLAMOURING FOR EXTREME MEASURES!

Now, Colonel, why not simply vaporise their entire lair with our atomic weapons and...

...at the same time annihilate the Swordfish and its secrets, right?... No, gentlemen, it is absolutely vital that we get our hands on that machine!... But don't worry, I know another way...

These weapons haven't been used yet, but I give you my word that before the sun rises, the Imperial flag will be flying over that scornful rock!

Oh, it's only a reprieve!... And you can bet your last penny that the Imperials are cooking up something nasty for tonight!... So we're counting on your Swordfish more than ever!

Radio, take note and transmit in code the order I'm about to dictate: "Colonel Olrik, commander of the expeditionary corps, on board carrier Kang-Hi, to Colonel Taksa, commander of the secret arsenal, Lhasa – stop – send two tons GX3 bombs immediately – stop – special mission, top priority – stop".

MEANWHILE, IN THE ASSEMBLY ROOM...

...Yes, old chap. Barring an accident, we'll be ready on schedule... In fact, after your victory we're all raring to go!

NIGHT FALLS AND THE HOURS SLOWLY TICK BY, HEAVY WITH DREAD. ON BOTH SIDES RADARS, DETECTORS AND PERISCOPES SEARCH THE NIGHT, EVER ATTENTIVE...

RETURNING FROM INSPECTING THE BATTERIES, SIR WILLIAM AND BLAKE ENTER THE LOOKOUT POST.

Anything new, Adam?

No, sir, apart from the arrival of three bombers an hour ago. They were coming from the east, north-east and landed on the Kang-Hi. Nothing since.

It's too quiet... I don't like it...

JUST THEN...

The Imperials are attacking!!!

THE ANTI-AIRCRAFT BATTERIES FILL THE AIR WITH LEAD AND STEEL, BUT THE ATTACK WAS LAUNCHED SO SUDDENLY THAT TWO OF THE BOMBERS, FLYING THROUGH THE MAN-MADE STORM, MANAGE TO SCORE SEVERAL DIRECT HITS... TO THE PERPLEXITY OF THE DEFENDERS, HOWEVER, THE PECULIAR BOMBS CAUSE NO EXPLOSIONS WHEN THEY BURST, BUT INSTEAD RELEASE AN ENORMOUS AMOUNT OF SMOKE. THE HEAVY CURLS UNFOLD AND CREEP OUTWARDS, SOON ENVELOPING THE ENTIRE BASE IN A HUGE GREENISH CLOUD...

THE DREADED CALL RESOUNDS...

Gas!!! It's a gas attack!!! Put on your masks!!!

THE ALERT SPREADS THROUGH THE BASE IN A FLASH, AND EVERY SOLDIER, ADJUSTING HIS MASK...

...GETS READY TO FACE THIS NEW OPPONENT WITH FIERCE DETERMINATION...

AT LAST THE INEVITABLE ORDER COMES!

All defensive positions!... Retreat! Fall back inside! Leave no man behind! Lock airtight hatches!... Hurry!...

ALAS! THE CHOKING SWIRLS SEEP THROUGH EMBRASURES AND OBSERVATION PORTS, RAPIDLY FILLING GUN EMPLACEMENTS AND BUNKERS. IT DOESN'T TAKE LONG FOR THE HORRIFIED DEFENDERS TO REALISE THAT THE FILTERS OF THEIR MASKS ARE POWERLESS TO STOP THAT SUBTLE POISON. SUFFOCATING, THE MEN COLLAPSE AND WRITHE ON THE GROUND, STRUGGLING DESPERATELY AGAINST THAT STRANGE, APPALLING FOE...

FORCED TO BEAT A HASTY RETREAT IN VIEW OF THE VIRULENCE OF THE 'GREEN GAS', THE DEFENDERS, CARRYING THEIR WOUNDED, WITHDRAW TO BASE, CLOSING BEHIND THEM THE HEAVY, AIRTIGHT STEEL DOORS.

Hello!... Things are taking a turn for the worse here, Mortimer!... Yes, some unknown gas... We're going to barricade every corridor and fight them for every inch of ground, but our already limited forces have suffered severe losses, so... Anyway, does your deadline still stand?...

Well, of course!!!... We're in the middle of connecting the oxygen generators... If you need to, concentrate the defence on the hall and the power plant. But for the love of God, Governor, hold!!!... Another 70 minutes!!!

BLAKE, WHO WAS WITH THE REARGUARD, NOW JOINS SIR WILLIAM, WHO COMMANDS THE DEFENCE OF THE ASSEMBLY ROOM.

I've set up staggered groups to harry the enemy all along the path that leads to this last barricade. The passages that can't be defended were mined...

Well, I do believe there's nothing more we can do, Blake!

FROM THE BRIDGE OF THE KANG-HI, OLRIK AND HIS STAFF INTENTLY FOLLOW THE OPERATIONS' PROGRESS...

Ha! Ha! They've stopped firing!... Good! Major, give the signal to the assault barges!

Yes, Colonel.

AND FOR THE SECOND TIME, BARGES HEAVY WITH TROOPS CONVERGE ON THE ENORMOUS ROCK, NOW SILENT...

UPON ARRIVAL, THE CRAFT LOWER THEIR BOW RAMPS AND THE SOLDIERS JUMP INTO THE WATER. PROTECTED BY THEIR SPECIAL MASKS, THEY ADVANCE SWIFTLY THROUGH THE ACRID SMOKE...

Captain, the enemy retreated inside after blocking the firing slits!

It doesn't matter, Lieutenant. Open a breach with explosives and use the flame-throwers to clean up!

IMMEDIATELY A GROUP OF SAPPERS HURRY FORWARD WITH THEIR EQUIPMENT AND BEGIN PIERCING A HOLE THROUGH THE COLOSSAL STONE WALL...

The final act has just begun, sir. Time is running out for the Swordfish!

No doubt... But whether we are victorious or defeated, I give you my word that if they get their hands on the Swordfish, it will be as scrap metal, dammit!!!

JUST THEN, THE MINE EXPLODES WITH A THUNDEROUS BANG, GUTTING A GUN EMPLACEMENT AND OPENING A LARGE BREACH...

THE DUST FROM THE EXPLOSION HAS BARELY BEGUN TO CLEAR BEFORE THE IMPERIALS ARE THROUGH THE BREACH, FLAME-THROWERS LEADING THE WAY...

THE HARRYING SQUADS OFFER BITTER RESISTANCE BUT THE ATTACKERS, WITH THEIR TERRIBLE WEAPONS, SCORCH EVERYTHING IN THEIR WAY, TAKE THE POSITIONS ONE AFTER THE OTHER AND FINALLY REACH THE LAST DOOR THAT BARS THE GALLERY LEADING TO THE ASSEMBLY ROOM. SOON IT TOO IS BLOWN OPEN...

Well, it's our turn now...

Even if Mortimer finishes on schedule, I'm afraid it will be too late!...

MOMENTS LATER, THE IMPERIALS, WALKING FORWARD WARILY, COME INTO VIEW AT THE END OF THE GALLERY ... AND THE SHOOTING STARTS...

Crikey! The more you shoot, the more keep on coming!

Yes, and if they manage to get close enough to use their flame-throwers, our goose will be well and truly cooked – and so will we!!!

My dear Blake, I don't think we should entertain any illusions of how this battle will end...Take command of the survivors and fall back towards the immersion chamber. Pick up Mortimer and his men as you go, as well as the ones from the power plant. In the meantime, I...

AT THAT MOMENT, THOUGH, THE LIGHTS GO OUT, PLUNGING THE ADVERSARIES INTO DARKNESS.

Dammit! A short circuit!

They must have hit the cables with their flame-throwers!

UNDER COVER OF THE DARKNESS AND DESPITE THEIR LOSSES, THE IMPERIALS KEEP CREEPING FORWARD. ALREADY SPARKS ARE BEGINNING TO FALL AMONG THE DEFENDERS, COMING DANGEROUSLY CLOSE TO AN AMMUNITION TRAIN WAITING BEHIND THE BARRICADE...

Heavens! Move these blasted wagons back!... If the fire reaches the ammo, we'll all go up in smoke!!!

We can't reverse, sir. The switch is stuck!

THEN NASIR SPEAKS UP...

Wait, sahib, I know a way!...

You, Nasir? How would you do it?

Well, I'd tell the sahib to send the train forward!

Great Scott! That's a smashing idea! Come on, boys, quick – clear up these rails!

OBSTACLES ARE REMOVED FROM THE TRACKS IN NO TIME, AND THE TRAIN IS MANOEUVRED INTO POSITION. BLAKE PUSHES THE HANDLE FORWARD AND THE WAGONS, SLOWLY GAINING SPEED, RUMBLE TOWARDS THE IMPERIAL LINES...

Bye-bye!!!

And now, boys, hit the deck quickly if you don't want to go heaven just yet!!!

SEEING THAT UNEXPECTED OPPONENT RUSH TOWARDS THEM, THE STARTLED IMPERIALS TAKE IT FOR A DESPERATE COUNTER-ATTACK OF THE BESIEGED AND IMMEDIATELY CONCENTRATE THE JETS OF THEIR FLAME-THROWERS ON THE THREAT...

THE RESULT IS PREDICTABLE. A BLINDING FLASH IS INSTANTLY FOLLOWED BY A DEAFENING EXPLOSION THAT OBLITERATES THE TRAIN AND EVERYTHING NEAR IT, CAUSING PART OF THE GALLERY TO COLLAPSE AND BLOWING DOWN THE BRITISH BARRICADE...

STUNNED, BRUISED AND BATTERED, BUT ALIVE, THE DEFENDERS PICK THEMSELVES UP FROM AMONG THE MASS OF SHATTERED DEBRIS, WHILE UNDERNEATH THE RUBBLE THE AMMUNITION CONTINUES TO GO OFF IN SUCCESSION...

Good grief! I think we got off easy!

Yes, and it's going to delay them for a good long time!

A VOICE RINGS OUT AMID THE DIN...

Professor Mortimer is calling for Captain Blake urgently!

At last!

Go on, Blake...and good

Thank you, sir. I won't let you down!

AND BLAKE DASHES OFF TOWARDS THE WORKSHOP...

May Allah protect you, sahib!

Goodbye, my friend!

SX-1

A LITTLE LATER, BLAKE ENTERS THE ASSEMBLY ROOM. BEFORE HIM, ALREADY SET ONTO THE MANOEUVRING CARTS AND SURROUNDED BY BUSY TECHNICIANS, ARE THE SX1 AND SX2, FIRST PROTOTYPES OF THE AIRCRAFT UPON WHICH DEPENDS THE FATE OF MILLIONS OF OPPRESSED PEOPLE: THE SWORDFISH!

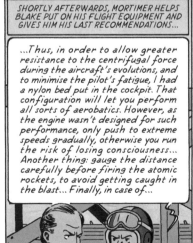

SHORTLY AFTERWARDS, MORTIMER HELPS BLAKE PUT ON HIS FLIGHT EQUIPMENT AND GIVES HIM HIS LAST RECOMMENDATIONS...

...Thus, in order to allow greater resistance to the centrifugal force during the aircraft's evolutions, and to minimise the pilot's fatigue, I had a nylon bed put in the cockpit. That configuration will let you perform all sorts of aerobatics. However, as the engine wasn't designed for such performance, only push to extreme speeds gradually, otherwise you run the risk of losing consciousness... Another thing: gauge the distance carefully before firing the atomic rockets, to avoid getting caught in the blast... Finally, in case of...

JUST THEN, A FOREMAN RUSHES TOWARDS MORTIMER...

Professor, one of the seals in the SX2's cockpit is leaking. It'll take us 15 minutes to sort out, maybe more...

Dammit!!!

Listen, old chap, time is of the essence. I'll go ahead and you join me as soon as possible... Besides, if I fail, your presence here is much more vital than mine...

Fine, but in that case stay in radio contact...

AND THE CAPTAIN, HAVING SAID HIS GOODBYES TO MORTIMER, SWIFTLY CLIMBS ABOARD THE SX1.

Cheerio, Mortimer!

Good luck, Blake!

45

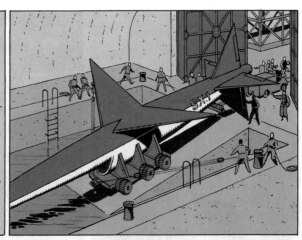

WHILE BLAKE STRAPS HIMSELF INTO THE COCKPIT, THE TECHNICIANS, FOLLOWING MORTIMER'S SIGNALS, HOOK A SMALL TRACTOR TO THE MANOEUVRING CART. THE STRANGE MACHINE IS IMMEDIATELY BROUGHT TOWARDS THE EXIT HATCH. PAST IT, THE MYSTERIOUS SWORDFISH, LIKE A GIGANTIC VERSION OF ITS NAMESAKE, ROLLS DOWN A SLOPED RAMP AND INTO THE WATER OF THE LOCK AS THE DOORS CLOSE BEHIND IT...

THE PROFESSOR TAKES CHARGE OF THE MANOEUVRE...

Ready on the pumps!

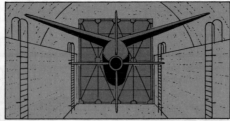

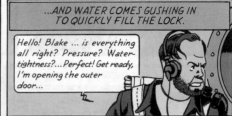

...AND WATER COMES GUSHING IN TO QUICKLY FILL THE LOCK.

Hello! Blake ... is everything all right? Pressure? Water-tightness?...Perfect! Get ready, I'm opening the outer door...

AND THE SWORDFISH, TRAVELLING ACROSS THE GREAT SUBMARINE LOCK, GLIDES THROUGH THE ENORMOUS STEEL DOOR THAT GUARDS THE BASE'S ENTRANCE AND EXITS INTO THE SEA...

CAREFULLY NEGOTIATING THE MINEFIELD OUTSIDE, BLAKE HEADS OUT TOWARDS OPEN WATERS, ATTEMPTING TO PINPOINT THE LOCATION OF ENEMY VESSELS WITH HIS DETECTION SYSTEMS...

Hello! Francis? Good news! Repairs on the SX2 are over. I'm on my way!... Oh, don't forget to shut off the oxygen tank when you emerge... And, more importantly, open the air intake!

Understood, old chap!... Ah, there's just the spot I was looking for. Well, Mortimer, goodbye, and God save England!!!

WITH THESE WORDS BLAKE RAISES THE NOSE OF THE AIRCRAFT AND PUSHES THE ENGINES TO FULL POWER. THE SWORDFISH, SPEED INCREASING GRADUALLY, LEAPS TOWARDS THE SURFACE, PUSHED BY ITS POWERFUL PROPULSION...

AT THAT MOMENT, THE IMPERIAL FLAG IS RAISED OVER THE BASE.

Well, gentlemen? Did I not keep my word?

46

OLRIK HAS NO SOONER FINISHED HIS SENTENCE THAN THE SWORDFISH ROCKETS OUT OF THE WATER IN A GREAT PLUME OF SPRAY...

...AND LEAPS TOWARDS THE SKY WITH A MIGHTY ROAR.

THEN, TURNING HARD, IT DIVES STRAIGHT TOWARDS THE HEAVY CRUISER KWEN LUN, WHOSE BEWILDERED GUNNERS STAND ROOTED AT THEIR POSTS, UNABLE TO ATTEMPT THE SLIGHTEST DEFENSIVE ACTION.

A HUNDRED YARDS FROM THE SHIP, THE SWORDFISH SUDDENLY LAUNCHES ONE OF ITS ATOMIC ROCKETS AT IT...

...AND WHILE THE COLOSSUS, HIT SQUARELY BY THE TERRIFYING PROJECTILE, BLOWS UP IN A TORRENT OF FLAMES...

...THE SWORDFISH HURRIES TOWARDS NEW VICTIMS.

SKIMMING THE WAVES LIKE A SPEEDBOAT, BLAKE FLIES UP THE LINE OF DESTROYERS, SMASHING THEM ONE AFTER THE OTHER AND LEAVING ONLY BURNING HULKS BEHIND...

...THEN, AFTER GAINING SOME ALTITUDE AND COMPLETING A VERTIGINOUS LOOP, HE DIVES TOWARDS THE AIRCRAFT CARRIER.

AT THAT MOMENT, BLAKE IS HORRIFIED TO DISCOVER THAT THE AIRCRAFT'S CONTROLS ARE NO LONGER RESPONDING...

What's happening?... Mortimer!... Mortimer!

...AND THE OUT-OF-CONTROL MACHINE IS RUSHING TOWARDS THE BASE AT DIZZYING SPEED...

The elevators are stuck! I've lost pitch control!!!!

Heavens!!!! The cockpit, quick!!! Eject the cockpit!!!! I'm coming!!!

47

SKIMMING THE WAVES LIKE A SPEEDBOAT, THE SWORDFISH FLIES UP THE LINE OF DESTROYERS, SMASHING THEM ONE AFTER THE OTHER AND LEAVING ONLY BURNING HULKS BEHIND...

WITHOUT HESITATION, BLAKE PULLS THE EJECTION LEVER. THE AIRCRAFT'S NOSE SEPARATES INSTANTLY, CAUSING THE AUTOMATIC EXPULSION OF THE PILOT FROM THE COCKPIT...

JUST IN TIME... FIVE SECONDS LATER, THE ABANDONED SX1 ENDS ITS COURSE AGAINST THE TOP OF THE BASE, EXPLODING ALONG WITH ITS REMAINING ATOMIC ROCKETS AND, IN A BLINDING FLASH, WIPING OUT THE TROOPS SCATTERED ACROSS THE ROCK'S SURFACE.

THE COLOSSAL DEFLAGRATION TURNS THE BASE INTO AN ENORMOUS BONFIRE. BLAKE, CAUGHT IN THE SHOCK WAVE, STRUGGLES TO COMPENSATE FOR THE EFFECTS OF THE SUDDEN WINDSTORM...

...BUT THE IMPERIALS HAVE OVERCOME THEIR SHOCK, AND THE ANTI-AIRCRAFT BATTERIES OF THE KANG-LI, SPARED THE DEVASTATION, BEGIN THUNDERING ANGRILY.

FORTUNATELY FOR THE CAPTAIN, THE SMOKE FROM THE BURNING SHIP HAMPERS THE GUNNERS CONSIDERABLY AND THEIR FIRE PROVES INEFFICIENT.

The fighters! Scramble the fighters, by thunder!

TAKING OFF IN HASTE, THE PLANES RUSH TO ATTACK...

...BUT AT THAT MOMENT THE SX2, RISING UP FROM THE BOTTOM OF THE OCEAN, PIERCES THE SURFACE OF THE WATER...

...AND, LEAVING A TRAIL OF FIRE BEHIND, SOARS UP INTO THE SKY TO MEET THE FIGHTERS.

IN LESS TIME THAN IS NEEDED TO WRITE IT, THE ENEMY SQUADRONS ARE SWATTED ASIDE, SMASHED, BLOWN TO PIECES AND LEAVE ONLY DEBRIS SCATTERED TO THE FOUR WINDS.

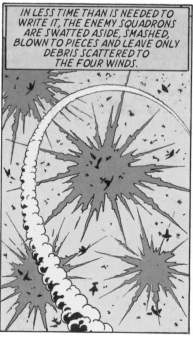

WHILE THE SX2 CLEARS THE SKY OF ENEMY AIRCRAFT, BLAKE, PUSHED TOWARDS THE SHORE BY A GUST OF WIND, IS PROMPTLY TARGETED BY THE GROUND-BASED ARTILLERY. SEEING THE DANGER, MORTIMER BANKS HARD AND DIVES...

FROM THE OBSERVATION DECK OF THE KANG-HI, OLRIK, LIVID WITH RAGE AND POWERLESS, FOLLOWS THE EVOLUTIONS OF THAT STRANGE AND TERRIBLE OPPONENT.

By the devil!... If they miss it, we're done for!

DESPITE THE ROCKETS THAT SHRIEK AROUND HIM, THE SWORDFISH SWOOPS STRAIGHT AT THE BATTERIES AND...

...INSTANTLY GUNNERS AND LAUNCHERS VANISH IN A HURRICANE OF FLAMES.

AT THE SIGHT, OLRIK DECIDES NOT TO WAIT ANY LONGER. HURRIEDLY DEPARTING FROM THE TOP DECK, HE DASHES TOWARDS A FIGHTER READY FOR TAKE OFF...

NOT A MOMENT TOO SOON!... ALREADY THE SX2 IS STARTING A NEW ATTACK RUN. DIVING FROM ON HIGH TOWARDS HIS LAST OPPONENT, MORTIMER LAUNCHES A VOLLEY OF ATOMIC ROCKETS STRAIGHT AT THE FLIGHT DECK. GUTTED, THE KANG-HI BLOWS UP JUST AS OLRIK LEAVES THE PLATFORM. THE PLANE IS MERCILESSLY BUFFETED BY THE EXPLOSION, BUT MANAGES TO RECOVER AND DISAPPEARS INTO THE SMOKE.

THEN, SKIMMING THE WAVES DOTTED WITH SMOKING WRECKS AND IGNORING THE FEW SURVIVING SHIPS THAT ARE FLEEING IN EVERY DIRECTION, MORTIMER PREPARES TO TOUCH DOWN ON THE SURFACE. BLAKE, WHO HAS JUST LANDED SAFE AND SOUND, CHEERS HIM AS HE PASSES.

AN HOUR LATER, FROM THE BASE'S EMITTER, SIR WILLIAM CALLS OUT TO THE WORLD...

Hello! Hello! This is the 'Free World'!... Hello! Hello! Calling all clandestine radio stations: an important message...

TODAY, THE IMPERIAL OPPRESSORS HAVE BEEN DEALT A CRUSHING BLOW THAT FORETELLS THEIR COMING DESTRUCTION. TWO PROTOTYPES OF A NEW AIRCRAFT CALLED THE SWORDFISH, BUILT IN A SECRET BASE IN THE SEA OF OMAN, HAVE JUST OBLITERATED ...

...AN ENTIRE EXPEDITIONARY CORPS THAT COMPRISED AIR, LAND AND SEA UNITS. A POWERFUL SQUADRON OF THESE TERRIBLE MACHINES IS ABOUT TO GO INTO ACTION. FREE MEN OF THE WORLD, THE TIME OF LIBERATION HAS COME! FIGHT THE INVADER!!!

MEANWHILE, MORTIMER ADDRESSES THE MEN OF THE ASSEMBLY ROOM...

...And now, to work, boys! We need a squadron before they've had time to recover.

DESPITE THE CENSORSHIP'S DESPERATE EFFORTS, NEWS OF THE DISASTER OF THE STRAIT OF HORMUZ HAS SPREAD LIKE WILDFIRE AND FILLED THE EMPIRE WITH DISMAY.

AT THE IMPERIAL PALACE, THE GREAT COUNCIL HAS BEEN IN SESSION FOR THREE WHOLE DAYS.

Yes, His Majesty's wrath is indescribable and he's decided to wipe out the rebels with the Lei Kong atomic missiles. To that effect, the Emperor has had the palace connected to the arsenal by a system that will allow him, when the time comes, to launch the strike himself at the simple press of a button. Only the presence of our troops on enemy soil has prevented him from carrying out his plan.

But why not nip the revolt in the bud? Let's vaporise the Swordfish in its lair!

Yes, but the information gathered about the devil's machine is so confused and the panic that followed the debacle is so great that the general staff decided to wait for Olrik's report before risking another attack. So, in the meantime, the air force simply kept an eye on the Strait area, which is how Olrik's plane was located only a few hours ago, immobilised after a forced landing among the cliffs of Makran. He's expected back any minute now.

MEANWHILE, THE EMPEROR, LOCKED INSIDE HIS OFFICE WITH DR SUN FO, IS LISTENING TO THE LATTER READING THE LATEST NEWS...

...Everywhere, whole armies of insurgents are rising up, well equipped with weapons and supplies hidden during the conquest. Paris, Madrid and Rome have been retaken by the rebels after heavy street fighting. New York: General Ogotai was forced to retreat to Coney Island with the remnants of his garrison. Buenos-Aires: the soldiers of the 8th Corps lost their morale and mutinied...'

...Shanghai: General Chang Li Chek rebelled and went over to the enemy with the 48th Armoured Division...'

Enough!!!

Traitors! Cowards! My own officers!... Well, all the better, then! There is no longer any obstacle between me and my vengeance and... But no! A sudden and unexpected death would be too good for them... I want them to know first. Fo!... Fo!... Patch me through to the global network and have it announce a special broadcast.

Yes, Your Majesty.

Ha! Ha! How can those pathetic worms be so arrogant as to rise against me...

...when, hidden deep inside the Yen Wang Ye valley, a thousand carriers of death await only a wave of my hand to leap into the skies!!!

But, most mighty Emperor, once your noble hand has sent forward all these unknown and terrible forces, is it not to be feared that the Empire will, in turn, be drawn into the catastrophe that your divine wrath will have provoked?...

Let the Empire perish, then!... But let my will be done!!!

O mighty Emperor, the line is connected!...

Ah!

Hello! Hello! This is Radio Lhasa bringing you a special broadcast!... Hello! Hello! Listen! Listen to your master; the great, the illustrious, the magnanimous Emperor Basam Damdu, from the heights of his unreachable greatness, deigns to address you...

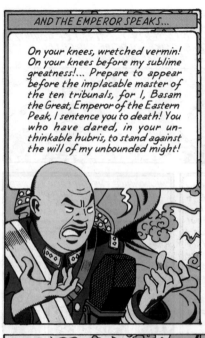

AND THE EMPEROR SPEAKS...

On your knees, wretched vermin! On your knees before my sublime greatness!... Prepare to appear before the implacable master of the ten tribunals, for I, Basam the Great, Emperor of the Eastern Peak, I sentence you to death! You who have dared, in your un-thinkable hubris, to stand against the will of my unbounded might!

In the valley of Yen Wang Ye, hundreds of missiles of terrifying power...

...await, pointed at every corner of the Earth. In mere moments, the fires of the Eighteen Hells will be upon you. And it is I, Basam Damdu, son of the great Kwan Ti, who will unleash them from the top of my throne. As for you, disloyal soldiers who betrayed me, the Black and White Wuchang need only my word to drag you down to the Ten Shi-Tien Yen-Wang! I have spoken, and may Lei Gong's bronze hammer crush you and turn you to dust!!!... There... I am now bringing my finger to the button and counting... One... Two...

Exalted Majesty, Colonel Olrik requests the honour of an urgent audience...

Ah!... I almost forgot about him!!! Show him in!

Sire, I miraculously survived the disaster and made my way back to Lhasa, with all speed, to place myself at Your Majesty's orders and assist you with my modest advice...

I expected no less of you!... And what is your advice, loyal servant?

Sire, smash the Swordfish's lair with our atomic weapons without delay! And as I have a personal score to settle with those people, I request the honour of launching the first missile!

You shall have your wish!

Guards! Seize that traitor and tie him to the first missile to be launched!!!

Sire!?!

BUT AT THAT MOMENT, THE SOMBRE WAIL OF THE ARSENAL'S SIREN RISES FROM THE DEPTH OF THE VALLEY...

FROM ONE END OF THE LAUNCH BASE TO THE OTHER, THE ANTI-AIRCRAFT BATTERIES UNLEASH A FURIOUS FIRE!...

HEARING THIS, THE STARTLED EMPEROR AND HIS GUARDS FREEZE ON THE SPOT...

What... What is the meaning of this noise?!?

It means, O mighty Monarch, that the Swordfish is flying over your Empire! Ha! Ha! Ha!

INDEED, DESPITE THE FRANTIC BUT FUTILE FIRE FROM THE ANTI-AIRCRAFT DEFENCES, A SQUADRON OF SWORDFISHES LED BY BLAKE AND MORTIMER FLIES OVER THE YEN WANG YE VALLEY...

THE EMPEROR, SENT INTO A RAGE BY OLRIK'S SARCASM, RUSHES TO THE BALCONY...

By all the demons of all the hells, shoot them down! Shoot them down!!!

Too late, Basam Damdu! Too late!... You should prepare yourself to appear before the infernal judge with honour!!!

What do you say, you dog? Too late?! Ha! Ha!... I still have time to take the planet down with me!!!

AND, INTOXICATED WITH HOMICIDAL MADNESS, THE EMPEROR RUSHES TO THE CONTROL PANEL...

I will annihilate you all!!!

BUT AT THAT EXACT MOMENT, THE BOMB DROPPED BY BLAKE EXPLODES!... LIKE A SIGHT FROM HELL ITSELF, THE SKY CATCHES ON FIRE, ANNIHILATING IN ONE FELL SWOOP EVERY MISSILE LINED UP INSIDE THE LAUNCH BASE. THE FIERY BREATH SWEEPS OVER THE IMPERIAL PALACE, WHICH COLLAPSES LIKE A HOUSE OF CARDS, AND THE PROUD CITY SPRAWLING AT ITS FEET LIGHTS UP LIKE A TORCH...

Mission accomplished – raid successful!

IN A VISION OF APOCALYPSE, THE TERRIBLE DESTRUCTION SPREADS THROUGH STEPPES AND VALLEYS, DEVASTATING THE COUNTRY FOR DOZENS OF MILES. ITS MISSION OVER, THE SQUADRON TURNS ROUND AND HEADS BACK TOWARDS ITS BASE WHILE BLAKE MAKES A TERSE REPORT.

WHEN THE NEWS REACHES THE BASE, IT AROUSES INDESCRIBABLE ENTHUSIASM...

Boys! The raid was successful! The city and the arsenal have been destroyed! Victory is ours!!!

Hip hip hurrah!

...AND THE RADIO IMMEDIATELY SENDS THIS EXHILARATING VICTORY REPORT OVER THE AIRWAVES...

Hello! Hello! This is the 'Free World'! Citizens of the world, our victory is complete!... Tonight, a large formation of Swordfishes commanded by Captain Blake and Professor Mortimer razed the capital city of the Yellow Empire and its terrible secret arsenal to the ground – just as the blood-thirsty tyrant Basam Damdu was about to unleash upon the planet the most horrific of devastations. Now deprived of leadership and supply lines, the few isolated pockets of resistance are already doomed to extermination!... Citizens of the world, you are free!!!

TWO HOURS LATER, THE VICTORIOUS SQUADRON RETURNS TO BASE, WELCOMED BY THE CHEERS OF THE GARRISON GATHERED ON THE GLORIOUS ROCK!

A MONTH LATER, IN LONDON...

Good Lord! So much ruin...

Yes, old chap. But we will rebuild! And, once more, civilisation's had the last word! Let's hope that it will be for good, this time!!!

THE

END

THE ADVENTURES OF BLAKE & MORTIMER

1-The Yellow "M"
EDGAR P. JACOBS

2-The Mystery of the Great Pyramid Part 1
EDGAR P. JACOBS

3-The Mystery of the Great Pyramid Part 2
EDGAR P. JACOBS

4-The Francis Blake Affair
VAN HAMME - BENOIT

5-The Strange Encounter
VAN HAMME - BENOIT

6-S.O.S. Meteors
EDGAR P. JACOBS

7-The Affair of the Necklace
EDGAR P. JACOBS

8-The Voronov Plot
SENTE - JUILLARD

9-The Sarcophagi of the Sixth Continent Part 1
SENTE - JUILLARD

10-The Sarcophagi of the Sixth Continent Part 2
SENTE - JUILLARD

11-The Gondwana Shrine
SENTE - JUILLARD

12-Atlantis Mystery
EDGAR P. JACOBS

13-The Curse of the 30 Pieces of Silver Part 1
VAN HAMME - STERNE - DE SPIEGELEER

14-The Curse of the 30 Pieces of Silver Part 2
VAN HAMME - AUBIN - SCHRÉDER

2013

2014

15-The Secret of the Swordfish Part 1
EDGAR P. JACOBS

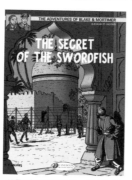

16-The Secret of the Swordfish Part 2
EDGAR P. JACOBS

17-The Secret of the Swordfish Part 3
EDGAR P. JACOBS

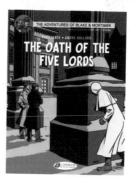

18-The Oath of the Five Lords
SENTE - JUILLARD

19-The Time Trap
EDGAR P. JACOBS

JACOBS
1946, the Swordfish, starting point of a masterful work

Article taken from the book: *The World of Edgar P. Jacobs* (Le Lombard publishers)

Cover of *Tintin* **magazine (November 28, 1946)**
© Edgar P. Jacobs

When, in 1946, daring publisher Raymond Leblanc decided to launch the magazine *Tintin*, Hergé called upon the services of his friend Jacobs. The latter proposed a medieval series, 'Roland the Bold', for which he wrote a complete script, but the project was discarded because there were already too many period costumed adventures in the magazine's layout.

Jacobs then proposed *The Secret of the Swordfish*, a futuristic series that was to open the cycle of Blake & Mortimer's adventures. The story was a great success with the public right from the start, and impressed many comic creators.

This episode was a reflection of the terrible conflict that had just ended with the terrifying destruction of Hiroshima and Nagasaki. Jacobs considered it a somewhat separate work. It was obvious that the Tibetan conquerors were really transposed Japanese, but page after page, Jacobs displayed unparalleled originality.

Regarding the technical side of dialogues, he eventually learnt, after some understandable trial-and-error, the proper placing of speech bubbles (the original publication of *The U Ray* didn't include any), eventually arriving, by the end of the second episode, at a chef-d'oeuvre of narrative figuration.

The unbalance between the end of the story and its beginning was such that, for its publication in graphic novel format, the author reworked the first 18 pages, even bringing them down to 17. Thus the lead-in became equally strong as the conclusion and, considering the end result, we can only agree with Jacobs' decision.

The Secret of the Swordfish reprised the idea of a submersible plane, which had first been seen at the beginning of the 20th century and was made popular by Jules Verne in *Master of the World* (1904). During the interwar period, the idea was used in the comic strip 'Tim Tyler's Luck' by Lyman Young, and even by Walt Disney with Mickey Mouse's 'submarplane'. There would however be two major differences between those stories and the *Swordfish*: the exemplary solidity of the script, and above all the design of the robotic machine, whose aerodynamic profile wasn't about to become outmoded any time soon.

To create the world-liberating machine, the conscientious Jacobs even hesitated between several devices, one of which was no less than an outstanding foreshadowing of the Polaris system! But in the end, it was the extraordinary white and blue Swordfish that won out – and still fascinates us today. This was a far cry from the approximate inventions that had come before Jacob's creation.

Correspondence between Claude le Gallo and Edgar P. Jacobs, November 20, 1967

In order to allow for the revenge and liberation of the nations defeated by the Yellow Empire's lightning attack, I had to find, besides a base of operations (the secret base of the Strait of Hormuz), a weapon that would be nigh invulnerable as well as powerful enough to neutralize the invaders' enormous war machine, but also sufficiently small and easy to handle to evade their hunt. Which immediately excluded any idea of a surface base or vehicle. Indeed we had no, or almost no, documentation on recent weapons – and next to nothing concerning nuclear weapons, rockets, radars, etc... We were still stuck with conventional armament and propeller planes... My first idea had considered four potential projects:

- A supersonic plane with a nuclear armament
- A ballistic missile submarine (that launched while submerged)
- An underwater missile base (at the bottom of a lake)
- A supersonic plane operating from an underwater base

I'd eventually opted for the submarine plane but, although it was very daring at the time, it still remained a classic type of vehicle – aside from having a jet engine, being designed for remote control and flying out of the water. Its behaviour once in the air was more or less that of a 'stuka'. Strangely enough, where I'd extrapolated with wild abandon in *The U Ray*, now the fear of going beyond credibility, coupled with my dislike for American-style science-fiction, had me positively paralysed. Until, in the course of discussing that situation with an old friend, he swept aside all my scruples and technical objections, encouraged me to move past this sudden faintheartedness and charge straight ahead into full-blown science-fiction (or rather what we still believed to be science-fiction!). In short, he managed to convince me, and then there was the Swordfish!

Once I'd accepted the principle, I launched into frenzied work. Keeping in mind, for the airframe, the different environments through which it would be called to perform – air and water – I made a series of very rough sketches and fairly quickly arrived at a silhouette that, to my eyes, seemed to meet the desired performance. Starting from there, I made a working drawing – plans, front view, side view, etc... – that I submitted for review to an expert in naval and aeronautical matters. Having concluded that no major impossibilities stood in the way of carrying out such a project, he built a model to scale. When I saw it, a name spontaneously came to my mind: swordfish! It had actually amply deserved that name, since I'd drawn inspiration from that fish's silhouette (as well as that of the shark) to create, from an aerodynamic standpoint, my machine's outline.

Model of the Swordfish
© Photos: Philippe Biermé

It is interesting to note that at the time that flying submarine was designed, a short-winged, slender-fuselage plane was not at all 'in'. On the contrary, the trend was all 'flying wings' and tail-less aircraft. I actually made a personal version of such an aircraft with Colonel Olrik's *Red Wing*. I'll mention also in passing the creation, still for the same story, of an Imperial fighter nicknamed the 'Flying Shark'. Seven years later, in 1953, the Americans unveiled an extraordinary plane, considered the most advanced of the time: the Douglas X3, which had a silhouette almost identical to that of the Swordfish. Finally – supreme accolade – 20 years later, the Americans announced the opening of an evaluation program between 44 manufacturers for a flying submarine project! And the US Navy clarified that this was in no way some science-fiction project; it deemed the existing technology sufficient to launch into the study of such a machine at that time.

DOUGLAS X3
© Science & Vie

Some technical details: the Swordfish was designed to be remote-controlled, and it was only under the pressure of events and running out of time that the heroes Blake and Mortimer, risking everything, took the extreme chance of flying the partially equipped aircraft themselves, taking the place of the remote-control mechanism.

The use and working of the controls are absolutely identical whether in flight or underwater. In flight, the engine's fuel feed is provided by the air. When diving, the air intake shuts off in contact with the water and automatically switches the circuit over to the oxygen tanks.

Note: the aircraft's nose drops off for pilot ejection.

Weapon load: infrared-guided, nuclear-tipped rockets and missiles.

DEATH IN THE PRESENT RE-AWAKENS A DARK TIME IN BLAKE'S PAST.

ANDRÉ JUILLARD

THE OATH OF THE FIVE LORDS

March 2014

TRANSLATED FOR THE FIRST TIME INTO ENGLISH

PUBLISHED BY

9th CINEBOOK
The 9th Art Publisher

YVES SENTE

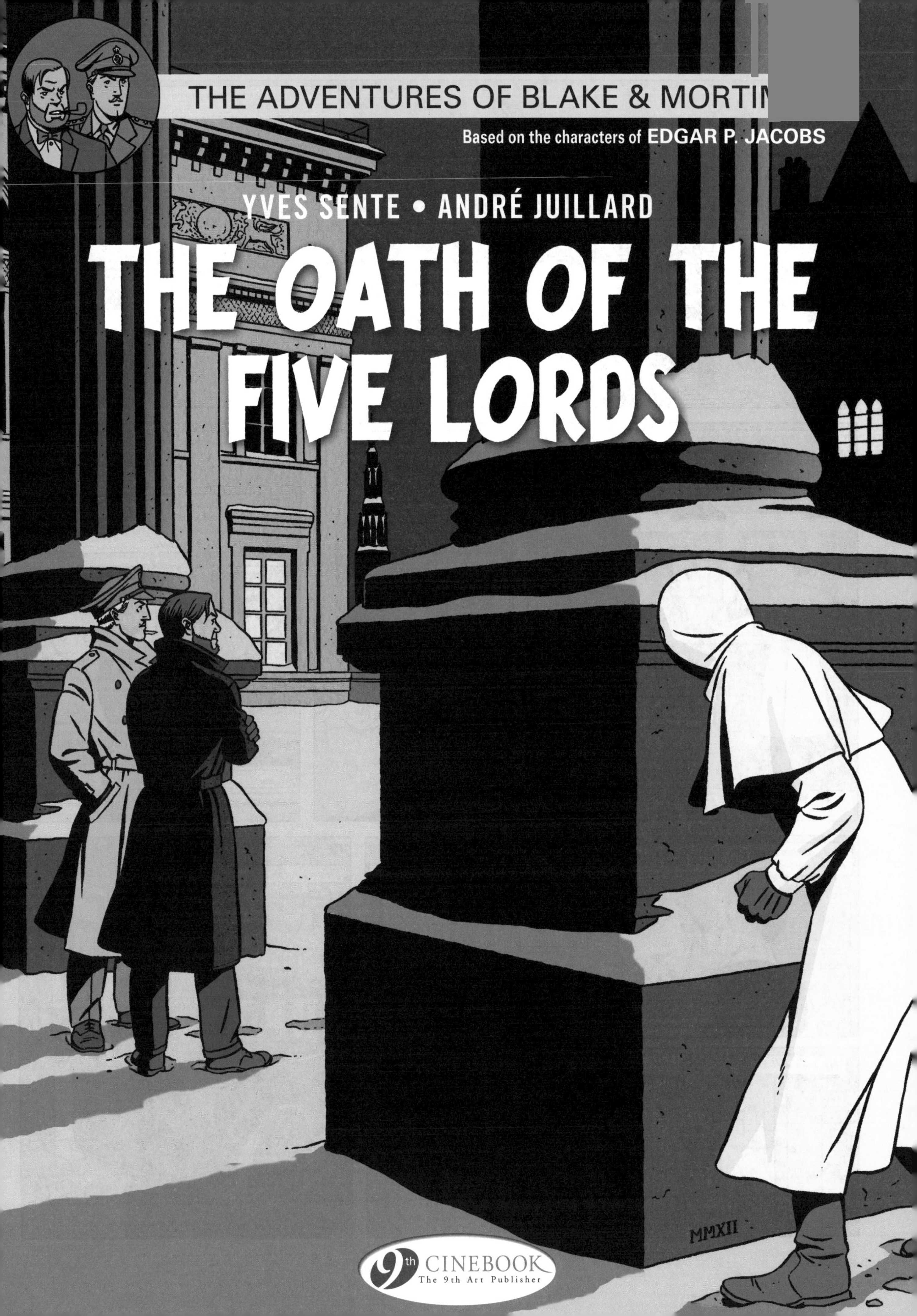
THE ADVENTURES OF BLAKE & MORTI
Based on the characters of EDGAR P. JACOBS
YVES SENTE • ANDRÉ JUILLARD
THE OATH OF THE FIVE LORDS
MMXII
CINEBOOK
The 9th Art Publisher

THE INHABITANTS OF BERKSHIRE WOULD LONG REMEMBER THAT MONTH OF NOVEMBER 1919 AS ONE OF THE COLDEST AND RAINIEST THE SOUTH OF ENGLAND HAD EVER KNOWN.

THAT EVENING, A MIX OF GLOOMINESS AND RESIGNATION COULD BE SEEN ON THE FACES OF THE FEW TRAVELLERS WAITING FOR A CONNECTION IN THE DAMP READING STATION.

My goodness! Will this rain ever stop pouring down? Barman, a double whisky! I feel like all this water has seeped through me all the way into my veins!

Aaaah! Blessed be our ancestors who invented this wonderful drink! I'd never have been able to board my connection to Bristol without this...

For Bristol, I doubt it. That train left ten minutes ago. But if you wait for the next one you'll have time to finish the bottle.

The London train is the last one tonight. To go to Bristol, you'll have to come back tomorrow.

Tomorrow?! But that's impossible! A taxi! I need a taxi!

My wife will kill me!

There's a phone box outside.

There's Peter. He's got the suitcase.

I'm not blind, Agent Carter!

THE OATH OF THE FIVE LORDS

1

THE OATH OF THE FIVE LORDS

Edgard Félix Pierre Jacobs (1904–1987), better known under his pen name Edgar P. Jacobs, was a comic book creator (writer and artist), born in Brussels, Belgium. It has been said of Jacobs that he didn't remember a time when he hadn't drawn.

Jacobs assisted fellow Belgian Hergé (Georges Prosper Remi) in the recasting of Hergé's *Tintin in the Congo, Tintin in America, King Ottokar's Sceptre* and *The Blue Lotus* for book publication. He also contributed directly to both the drawing and storylines for the Tintin double-albums *The Secret of the Unicorn/Red Rackham's Treasure* and *The Seven Crystal Balls/Prisoners of the Sun*.

When the comics magazine Tintin was launched on 26th September 1946, it included Jacobs' story *Le secret de l'Espadon* (*The Secret of the Swordfish*). This story would be the first in the Blake and Mortimer series.

The characters of Captain Francis Blake, dashing head of MI5, his friend Professor Philip Mortimer, a nuclear physicist, and their sworn enemy Colonel Olrik became legendary heroes of the 9th art in the long-running series.

After Jacobs' death in 1987, Bob de Moor completed his unfinished last story. In the mid-1990s, the series was continued by the Jacobs Studios with new teams of writers and artists.

ORIGINAL FRENCH EDITION		
1	1950	Le secret de l'Espadon, T1
2	1953	Le secret de l'Espadon, T2
3	1953	Le secret de l'Espadon, T3
4	1954	Le mystère de la Grande Pyramide, T1
5	1955	Le mystère de la Grande Pyramide, T2
6	1956	La marque Jaune
7	1957	L'énigme de l'Atlantide
8	1959	S.O.S. Météores
9	1962	Le piège diabolique
10	1967	L'affaire du collier
11	1971	Les trois formules du professeur Satō, T1
12	1990	Les trois formules du professeur Satō, T2 (Jacobs/De Moor)
13	1996	L'affaire Francis Blake (Van Hamme/Benoit)
14	2000	La machination Voronov (Sente/Juillard)
15	2001	L'étrange rendez-vous (Van Hamme/Benoit)
16	2003	Les sarcophages du Sixième Continent, T1 (Sente/Juillard)
17	2004	Les sarcophages du Sixième Continent, T2 (Sente/Juillard)
18	2008	Le sanctuaire du Gondwana (Sente/Juillard)
19	2009	La malédiction des 30 deniers, T1 (Van Hamme/Sterne/De Spiegeleer)
20	2010	La malédiction des 30 deniers, T2 (Van Hamme/Aubin)
21	2012	Le serment des cinq Lords (Sente/Juillard)

CINEBOOK EDITION		
15	2013	The Secret of the Swordfish, Part 1
16	2013	The Secret of the Swordfish, Part 2
17	2013	The Secret of the Swordfish, Part 3
2	2007	The Mystery of the Great Pyramid, Part 1
3	2008	The Mystery of the Great Pyramid, Part 2
1	2007	The Yellow "M"
12	2012	Atlantis Mystery
6	2009	S.O.S. Meteors
19	2014	The Time Trap
7	2010	The Affair of the Necklace
		Professor Satōs Three Formulas, Part 1
		Professor Satōs Three Formulas, Part 2
4	2008	The Francis Blake Affair
8	2010	The Voronov Plot
5	2009	The Strange Encounter
9	2011	The Sarcophagi of the Sixth Continent, Part 1
10	2011	The Sarcophagi of the Sixth Continent, Part 2
11	2011	The Gondwana Shrine
13	2012	The Curse of the 30 Pieces of Silver, Part 1
14	2012	The Curse of the 30 Pieces of Silver, Part 2
18	2014	The Oath of the Five Lords